the
Hurt
that they
Feel

the Hurt *that they* Feel

*Helping Preschoolers Deal
With Tough Issues*

Compiled by Rhonda R. Reeves

new
hope
PUBLISHERS

Birmingham, Alabama

New Hope® Publishers
P. O. Box 12065
Birmingham, AL 35202-2065
www.newhopepublishers.com

Library of Congress Cataloging-in-Publication Data
The hurt that they feel : helping preschoolers deal with tough issues / compiled by Rhonda R. Reeves.
p. cm.
Includes bibliographical references.
ISBN 1-56309-839-3 (softcover)
1.   Parenting-Religious aspects-Christianity. 2. Preschool children-Religious life. 3. Parent and child-Religious aspects-Christianity. I. Reeves, Rhonda R., 1952-
BV4529.H87 2004
248.8'45—dc22
2004013343

ISBN: 1-56309-839-3

N044120 • 0904 • 6M1

Contributors

- Susan Allen

- Sue Bredekamp

- Darla Botkin

- Karen Dockrey

- Jim Greenman

- Stanley I. Greenspan

- Grace Ketterman

- Bruce D. Perry

- Donna S. Quick

- Sam Quick

- Fred Rogers

- Hedda Sharapan

- Joye Smith

Table of Contents

Introduction

I began teaching school in 1974 when the lives of children seemed fairly uncomplicated and rather sensible. We had just begun to understand various learning disabilities and we delved into new methodologies and educational principles to rejuvenate public schools. Schools were safe and for most of us our homes were our refuge. "AIDS" were parent volunteers who helped us teachers. Most families were not blended, sandwiched, or split, and the church was still revered as the place to be on Sundays.

But by the time I left the classroom nearly two decades later, I realized life had begun to change and change drastically and rapidly. And whether these changes were good or bad, they were vastly impacting the future of our children.

As I talked to children's advocates, parents, caregivers, and teachers, most agreed that these changes had brought about some really tough issues that we as responsible adults must address for the sake of our little ones. However, many of these issues are striking our children and adults with such intensity that often a sense of helplessness and hopelessness envelops us.

Although concerned adults may have an overwhelming burden and sense of urgency to deal with these tough issues, they must recognize the need to be properly equipped with skills and information. The contributors to *The Hurt That They Feel* have offered us a wealth of knowledge. Throughout the book, these experts have presented advice and suggestions to help you deal with tough issues such as the spiritual development of young children, various family situations, illnesses and death, violence, conflict resolution, and appropriate learning. Each topic is aimed at helping adults understand the problem, find a solution, reflect on ways they can help, and then apply what they have learned.

Although times have changed, there's one thing for sure— our children still need us, now more than ever. When we all join together to deal with these tough issues, we can better provide for our children's happiness and safety. We can discover appropriate ways to help them solve conflicts; cope with sickness and death; teach them to love, respect, and trust each other; and lead them into a personal relationship with Jesus Christ and to know Him as their Lord and Savior.

As you read and study this book and begin to deal with the hurts children feel, my prayer is that God will empower you with His Holy Spirit to move in a mighty way for His children.

Rhonda R. Reeves

Chapter 1

Spiritual Development of Young Children

by Joye Smith

Three-year-old James and I talked about what we would do on our next day off and conversation turned to the beach. James expressed that he did not want to go to the beach because there was too much water and the water is salty. Then little James asked the impossible question, "Who put that salt in the water?"

I immediately answered that God puts the salt in the ocean water. I then realized that in James' literal thinking, he was seeing God as this big person with a giant salt shaker. What I thought was a simple answer turned out to leave a confusing image within the preschooler's mind.

I could have given an answer about the physics of our land and water, but I wanted to instill thoughts of God within this young mind. Helping young children learn about God is a tough issue.

The Dilemma

A concern for Christian parents and teachers at church is the question of how to guide a preschooler in his or her spiritual development. We know the love that Christ has given to us and want our children to know of Christ's love also. We want our children to "grow in the grace and knowledge of our Lord and Savior Jesus Christ" (2 Peter 3:18 NIV[1]). But our dilemma is in knowing how to lead children spiritually at such a young age.

What can a child understand spiritually? How much can we teach a young child about God? How early in life can a child know spiritual concepts and sense spiritual attitudes? When does faith development begin? These are among many questions posed by parents and church leaders. The place to start searching for answers is by looking at the child and the needs of preschoolers.

The Preschooler's Needs

The main task in the early years of life is the development of trust. A sense of trust begins in infancy as the child's physical and emotional needs are met. An infant or toddler will develop trust when his physical needs of food, changing, and sleep are met. The child comes to trust when his emotional needs are met, too. These emotional needs are filled when parents or caregivers talk with the infant, hold him close, rock him, or smile at him. When the child knows that his needs will be met, he begins to have a sense of trust in the adults who care for him and give him nurture.

The preschooler's trust for caregivers developed in early

childhood is the same type of trust that the child may have in God later in his life. Trust is the foundation on which other spiritual development is built. V. Bailey Gillespie expresses that trust "provides the basis of all religious tasks in the future life of individuals."[2] When a child trusts in those around him to love and care for him, it is easy to have the same trust that God loves and cares for us.

Parents have the major role in promoting the development of trust in their preschooler. Teachers at church also encourage trust with their consistency and love for the child. As the young child's needs are met, there is a positive effect on the trust instilled within the preschooler. The first years of life are important in building a relationship of trust in young children.

The preschool child also has the need for love from the moment she is born. The need for love is especially important for young children as they are dependent on adults for their well being. As a sense of self is developing, the child needs to know that she is loved. A child needs love that is nurtured in a warm and caring relationship. Relationship is the most important thing.

The preschooler's need for love is fulfilled when she is in a loving relationship with parents or caregivers. The loving relationship is defined not so much by what is done but by the attitude of love that is shown to the child. The old saying, "it is caught more than taught," runs true here. Preschoolers will know a loving attitude through the closeness shared, eye contact, facial expressions, and tone of voice. Young children come to know of God's love through the love shown by caring adults.

Christian parents and Sunday school teachers can model

attitudes about God, Jesus, the Bible, and church. The child will come to know the attitudes of respect, thankfulness, awe, love, and wonder. This is the foundation on which other religious concepts will be built later in life. The preschooler knows what a loving God is like through the attitudes of and relationships with loving adults. Bruce Powers gives testimony of the influence of his parents and Sunday School teachers in his early years. Powers recounts, "I can't remember too much about *what* they taught me; but I do remember how much they cared for and loved me."[3]

Nurturing children in spiritual development is important, but how early do we begin? V. Bailey Gillespie states, "Most parents begin to become interested in the religious life of their children around 5–9 years of age. This is exactly 5–9 years too late."[4] The early years of life are critical in the development of value systems and attitudes. Gillespie further states that these are the years that preschoolers develop their attitudes and stance toward God and life.

Miranda and her grandmother came to the early worship service and Sunday school. The second worship service of the church was broadcast over television. When the grandmother and child arrived home, they watched the service on television as the grandmother prepared lunch for the family. Three-year-old Miranda watched as the choir sang. When the pastor stood to preach Miranda said, "There's God." Miranda had seen the pastor many times at church as he visited the preschool area each Sunday. He spoke to her every Wednesday night at the church family dinner. She had come to associate him with church and with God. Our example can point a preschool child to God.

From a young age preschoolers need us to guide them toward God by our actions, attitudes, and words. Gary Oliver states, "A strong, consistent, Christ-centered, love-based relationship with our kids that helps them know they are loved, accepted and understood is the environment in which the 'Good News' of the gospel will be caught and not just taught."[5] A parent holds an infant close and hums "Jesus Loves Me." A teacher lovingly takes a toddler's hand when he's learning to walk. A three-year-old looks in wonder at a seashell that God made. A five-year-old imitates by telling a Bible story to a favorite doll. Beginning early, from infancy, to guide a child toward God and build on this foundation as the child grows is important.

Looking for a Solution

The Scriptures provide help for giving spiritual guidance to young children. The passage of Deuteronomy 6:4–9 gives the following instructions: "Hear, O Israel: The LORD our God, the LORD is one. Love the LORD your God with all your heart and with all your soul and with all your strength. These commandments that I give you today are to be upon your hearts. Impress them on your children. Talk about them when you sit at home and when you walk along the road, when you lie down and when you get up. Tie them as symbols on your hands and bind them on your foreheads. Write them on the doorframes of your houses and on your gates."

We see from the above passage that the most important part of guiding the spiritual development of preschoolers is in our own relationship with God. First we must know God and experience faith in Him as Lord. His love must saturate our own lives. Through faith in God we believe in Christ as our Savior. As we seek to know God and more of His love, we are drawn closer to Him. In seeking to be more like Christ, our relationship with Him will grow deeper in love. This love in our hearts is then what we will impress on our children.

The passage in Deuteronomy then tells us how to impress God's love on our children. We are to teach spiritual concepts through our daily lives at home and out in the world. We are to show God's love to children through the things that we do each day, from getting up to lying down. Our daily lives are to reflect God's love. God is to be in our thoughts, words, and actions. In our coming and going each day we are to point children to God, who loves them.

God is to be so much a part of our lives that teaching our children about Him is a natural part of our daily lives. We must be intentional about teaching preschoolers about God. This means taking the things we do every day and using them as tools to teach preschoolers about God. Talk to the preschooler about God and Jesus throughout the day, in play and in routine activities. Spiritual concepts can be taught through the activities in which preschoolers are involved. Many teachable moments come from the activities of preschoolers.

The wonderful thing about preschoolers is that many times they are doing or seeing something for the first time. They have so much excitement because everything is so new to them. This gives opportunities to teach them about God, His world, and His love. One class of two-year-olds took a nature walk. They were to look for leaves and grass, but as they were outside, a rainbow encircled the sky. The preschoolers were struck with awe as some had never seen a rainbow before except in a book. What an opportunity to tell them that God makes the sunlight, the rain, and the rainbow. What a good time to talk of how God cares for each of us. These teachable moments help preschoolers know God.

When one of those teachable moments comes along, tell the preschooler about God, Jesus, the church, or the Bible. God will become real to the preschooler when the child associates God with his activities throughout the day. Our actions and attitudes will show preschoolers our faith, and we must accompany this by using our words to tell them about our faith. The psalmist says, "We will tell the next generation the praiseworthy deeds of the LORD, his power, and the wonders he has done" (Psalm 78:4).

Learning about God

Preschoolers learn through using their senses. They learn by touching an item, smelling a flower, hearing a noise, or seeing an object. Those who work with babies know that they learn through taste because everything goes to their mouths. Adults can help preschoolers learn about God through their senses by relating sensory experiences to God. When a child smells different scents, give thanks to God for a nose to smell. Use the sense of hearing by playing songs that tell of Jesus' love. Let the child handle objects, and tell him, "God made you. God gave you hands to touch."

Another way preschoolers learn is through imitation. Preschoolers need caregivers who are examples of Christ. Teachers and parents point a child to God by modeling a Christ-like attitude. Adults are examples as they seek to live a life that honors God. Preschoolers imitate adults who treat others in loving ways and who seek to obey God. Teachers and parents serve as a model in patience, forgiveness, love, kindness, and trust in God. Teachers and parents can model how to love others, what to do when angry, and how to help other people. In Ephesians 5:1, Paul says to "Be imitators of God, therefore, as dearly loved children." As adults imitate Christ, preschoolers are given an example of the qualities of Christ.

Repetition is one of the ways that preschoolers learn about God. Preschoolers will come to know that God is real when they hear of God repeatedly throughout their daily lives. They will *not* know God if they hear of Him just one time. Speak about God as the child is doing everyday activities. Voice prayers to God during the day. Use a Bible with pictures to tell Bible stories to the child. Repeat these stories and the Bible verses used with preschoolers. Preschoolers like to hear stories over and over again. Repetition does not need to be in a rote manner, which the child repeats after you, but as a part of their activities. They learn through this repetition.

Using the Bible

One aspect of telling preschoolers of God is in using the Bible with them. Preschoolers need to sense that the Bible is a special book. They need to see adults using the Bible in their daily lives. Preschoolers need to have opportunities to hold the Bible and turn the pages as they see the printed words. Teachers can use the Bible by showing a preschooler a verse and saying, "This is where the Bible says that God loves me." Hold the Bible in your lap or within reach of preschoolers. Show how to handle the Bible in a careful manner. Express to the child that the Bible is a special book.

Preschool teachers and parents can use Bible thoughts and Bible conversation throughout activities with preschoolers. Bible thoughts are verses that are stated in a way that the preschool child can understand. As Thomas added ingredients to a fruit salad, the teacher said, "Thanks for using your hands to help. The Bible says, 'Work with your hands.'" Use these teachable moments to say a Bible thought to a preschooler. In this way the verse will have meaning to the child.

As the preschooler's attention span grows, he is able to listen to the stories of the Bible. Telling these stories is a way of sharing the biblical message with preschoolers. Bruce Powers lists telling and retelling the biblical story as a basic action in passing on faith.[6] The Bible tells of God and His Son, Jesus. It tells of His creation and His works in the world. The Bible depicts our rich heritage of those who have gone before us in faith in God. Young children need to hear these stories over and over again.

Bible stories need to be told in a clear, simple manner. Consider the child's level of understanding when choosing stories. The content of the story should be appropriate for the child's learning ability. Choose stories with meaning to the child. The best way to do this is to relate the story to what the child is doing. The child will have greater understanding of the story when it relates to his real life experiences.

Be sure to express not only the facts about the story, but also the feelings. The story of Jesus' entry into Jerusalem teaches about joy. The story of Zacchaeus teaches about forgiveness. The story of David and Jonathan teaches about friendliness. Portray the expression of feelings in the story through your tone of voice, eye contact, and facial expressions.

Preschoolers can be actively involved as Bible stories are told. Give children a repeated sound to listen for or an action to do at a certain point. Involve preschoolers in making a sound in the story. For the story of Mary and Joseph riding into Bethlehem on a donkey, preschoolers can help by making the "clop, clop, clop" sound of the donkey's hooves. Older preschoolers enjoy acting out the parts of characters in a familiar Bible story.

These points about telling Bible stories are also true when telling stories about missionaries. Tell preschoolers about missions work by telling of things that relate to their experiences. Tell of people with whom the preschooler can identify. Preschoolers can relate to issues of family, friends, housing, food, games, church, and occupations of missionaries. As a preschooler builds in the block area of the preschool room, a teacher tells the story of a church building that a missionary helped build. Help the child identify with stories about missions and the people involved.

Using Prayer

Prayer is another way of teaching preschoolers about God. Loving adults can lead the preschool child toward God by praying with the child. "The gift of prayer is the greatest inheritance we can give our children," writes Denise George in *Kids Can Talk to God*. "By teaching them to pray, we help them develop a natural, conversational relationship with God that will grow as they mature in their faith."[7] Teachers and parents can model prayer by talking to God throughout their daily experiences.

Like Bible stories that are told, the prayers spoken with the preschooler should relate to the experiences of the child. When prayers relate to the child's activities he comes to view prayer as an important part of his life. Find opportunities during daily activities to pray with the preschooler. Use short, simple sentences in prayers. At first these prayers may be a sentence prayer while holding an infant. For older preschoolers prayer includes thanksgiving to God, prayers for self, and prayers for others.

Model for preschoolers an attitude of prayer rather than giving the child a set formula for prayer. Using prayer in the child's daily life models an attitude of prayer. When my nephew Travis was a two-year-old, he enjoyed saying the blessing before meals. His open-eyed prayers gave thanks for each food item on the table. Prayer was meaningful to Travis as he looked at the table before him and expressed his thanks. Prayers can be used not only at meals and bedtime, but also throughout the day. On the ride home from the park a parent prays, "I thank God for the good time we had today." Or when a child's friend is not feeling well a teacher says, "Let's pray that Kirsten will feel better tomorrow." Such prayers teach preschoolers that we can talk with God at any time.

Listen to your child and give him opportunities to pray. The preschooler may be interested in talking to God in his own way. His prayers will have meaning to him when the child is encouraged to use his own words in prayer. Help the child to know that prayer does not require any fancy words, but a sincere heart. We can talk to God as naturally as we talk to another loved one. Our prayers with the child will teach him about our faith and will give an example of living out our faith.

Talking with Preschoolers

Being with preschoolers is a challenging experience because we do have to think about the way we communicate with preschoolers. Young preschoolers have a limited vocabulary and limited understanding. Much of the communication is nonverbal. The tone of voice, facial expression, and body stance tells the child if an adult is tense, relaxed, angry, happy, or joyful. The preschooler needs to hear the name of Jesus spoken in loving ways. When the body language of the adult matches the words spoken, the child knows the words are true. Even though the infants or toddlers may not understand everything that is said, they need to begin hearing about God and Jesus from an early age. Tell an infant that God made him. Talk in a gentle voice. Smile when talking about God. Sing a song about God to a toddler. Clap the rhythm of the words from a Bible thought with a one-year-old. Let the child hear words of thanks to God.

As the age of the preschooler increases, his ability to listen and comprehend increases, too. This gives many possibilities for talking about God in various ways. Tell a three-year-old short stories of Jesus and other people in the Bible. Give praise to a four-year-old for his efforts. Sing songs the five-year-old learns at church. Talk with the child in a loving manner.

Before the age of seven, the child thinks literally about the words that are spoken. A preschooler thinks that you literally mean what you say. Many stories illustrate this, such as the boy who drew Mary and Joseph with baby Jesus on an airplane. His teacher had told about Mary and Joseph's flight to Egypt. The child thought literally of a flight on an airplane. He is not able to think in terms of symbolism. For the child to comprehend, the words have to relate to something the child already knows. This is why preschoolers do not understand figures of speech. They do not yet have the mental capability to think in abstract phrases.

Teachers and parents need to consider the concrete thinking of the preschooler when talking with the child. Avoid using symbolic terms such as the "house of God." A preschooler would know this as "church." Many times adults are so accustomed to the "churchy" words used that we forget to think of how the preschooler comprehends the words. Use words that do not have symbolic meaning. Realize that the child thinks in the here and now. Use religious songs that do not use symbolism or abstract ideas. A child will understand the phrase, "tell others about Jesus," much more than "shine your light on the world." By thinking of the words used with the preschooler, teachers and parents can decrease the child's confusion about God.

Spiritual Concepts

What can a preschool child come to know about spiritual things? What are some concepts that can be taught to the preschool child? Let's take a look at the areas that a preschooler learns about spiritual concepts. Eight different areas serve as a focus in teaching preschoolers spiritual concepts. What does a preschooler learn in each of these areas?

God

The preschooler needs to know that *God loves him. God wants us to love others and be kind to them. I can talk to God. God wants us to tell others about Him.* These are truths that are conveyed to the child by speaking of God and relating to the preschooler in a warm and loving manner.

A teacher softly says to an infant, "God loves you and cares for you." As two older preschoolers work together on an art activity, a teacher states, "God is glad when we work together." Preschoolers need to sense God's love and care in their daily lives. The child needs to associate God with happy experiences. One day a father planted tomato plants outside along with his two-year-old son, Jonathan. In talking with the child, the father said that God would help the plant to grow and red tomatoes to grow on the plant. Some time later when they picked the ripe tomatoes, Jonathan held a tomato and said, "God." The father responded, "Yes, God helped the tomato to grow." The father was amazed that the child had remembered what was said in the midst of their activity.

Jesus

The preschooler learns that *Jesus was a baby; He grew to be a boy and then a man. Jesus is God's Son. Jesus loves every person. Jesus helped people. Jesus had friends who loved Him. Jesus wants people to love and help each other.*

The preschooler needs to associate the name of Jesus with feelings of love and happiness. The child needs to hear parents and teachers at church talk about Jesus' love. Tell the child Jesus' name. Repeatedly tell the child Jesus loves him. Talk about Jesus as a friend and helper. Tell preschoolers the stories of Jesus from the Bible and say Bible thoughts about Jesus. Relate facts about Jesus to the activities of the child today. For example, while driving to church, tell the story of Mary and Joseph taking Jesus to church when He was a baby. Tell of Simeon and Anna, who were people at church who were glad to see Baby Jesus. Relate that the teachers at your church love and care for the child.

Bible

The preschooler comes to know that *the Bible is a special book. The Bible tells about God and Jesus. The Bible tells us that God and Jesus love us. The Bible also tells about people who loved God and Jesus. Some Bible stories tell how people told others about Jesus.*

Preschoolers learn that the Bible is a special book when they see its importance to parents and teachers. Preschoolers need to have many opportunities to use the Bible. Allow the preschooler to handle the Bible as he hears Bible songs and Bible thoughts. Help the child associate the Bible with stories about God and Jesus. The Bible will be meaningful to the preschooler as it relates to his life. Tell the stories of the Bible, point to pictures of Bible stories, and allow the child to hold the Bible. Model the importance of the Bible by using it in everyday activities.

Church

A preschooler learns that *people at church love me. People at church talk about God, Jesus, and the Bible. People at church help others. People use the Bible at church. People give money at church. I have friends at church.*

Preschoolers need to have a sense of love and security about church. They need to have positive experiences at church with teachers who are examples of God's love. Consistency of teachers at church is especially important for the early years as the child develops relationships with those who care for him. A preschooler gains a sense of belonging when people at church accept him and meet his needs.

Self

The preschooler needs to know that *God made me. I am special to God and God loves me. I am growing and can do many things.*

A preschooler needs to know that he is important to God. God made him as a unique person. Each preschooler needs to feel that he is accepted and loved. Provide a warm, accepting atmosphere for the child. Express thanks to God for the preschooler. Provide a secure environment in which the child feels love from others. Treat each child as an individual. The preschool years are an important time of building the child's self image.

Others

A preschooler learns that *each person is important to God. I can love and help others. Other people love me. Each person can do different things. Other people are alike in some ways and different in some ways. I can get along with others.*

As the preschooler matures, he comes to see the importance others have in his life. He learns the importance of communication and cooperation with others. The preschooler needs support and guidance as he develops relationships with family members, friends, and other adults in his life. Model a caring relationship with others so preschoolers will learn by example. Provide for pleasant experiences with other children and adults. The atmosphere at church needs to be an inviting setting in which the child feels secure in his relationships with others.

Family

The preschooler needs to know that *God planned for families. I have a family. My family loves me and takes care of me. Family members help each other. Families work and play together.*

Each child needs to feel that he belongs as a member of his family. Each child is in a unique family situation as the composition of each family is different. A preschooler learns about being a part of a family through the activities the family does together. Teachers at church partner with the family in helping the preschooler grow spiritually, physically, mentally, emotionally, and socially.

Natural World

A preschooler learns that *God made the world. God made plants, animals, the sun, moon, stars, and people. God planned for things to grow. God wants people to enjoy His world and take care of the natural world.*

Opportunities to guide a preschooler toward God through learning about God's creation abound. A preschooler needs the chance to use his senses to explore the natural world. Give opportunities to touch, taste, smell, hear, and see objects from nature. Parents and teachers can use these opportunities to express the awe and wonder of the world God made. Let the child hear you give thanks to God for His marvelous world.

Responsibilities and Blessings

Parents and church leaders want children to know about God, Jesus, and the Bible. Some teaching of spiritual concepts is intentional, such as directly telling a child a verse from the Bible. Most of the teaching that takes place is through modeling our relationship with God. Parents and teachers direct preschoolers toward God by being an example of God's trustworthiness. In meeting the child's physical and emotional needs the adult provides an atmosphere where trust can grow. When the child feels secure in relationships with others, he comes to know God is with me and takes care of me. The trust developed by the child is the foundation of the trust he may later have in Christ as Savior.

Above all else the greatest thing we can do for young children is to show them God's love. Gillespie says that "the greatest motivation for all of life is found in the fact that God is love."[8] God's love is the basis from which everything else can be found. Accepting a preschooler and loving him unconditionally are ways of showing him God's love. In this way we are laying the groundwork for future experiences of faith in God's unconditional love. What a difference we will make in the lives of young children when we help them to experience and know of God's love.

Guiding young children in their spiritual development is both an awesome responsibility and a blessing. We have the responsibility of modeling a Christ-like life for our children. Parents and teachers need to rely on God to mold their own lives to be an example of Christ. The blessings are abundant in sharing with preschoolers the love and joy God brings to our lives.

Application and Reflection

1. Think of a relationship you have with a preschooler.

2. How can you help the preschooler develop a sense of trust and love?

3. In what ways are you an example of God's love to the preschooler?

4. What qualities of God do you model for the child?

5. What are some ways that your church can lead preschoolers in developing trust?

6. Think of times that you can use the Bible with a child.

7. What are some ways that you model prayer to a preschooler?

8. How do your daily or routine experiences help a preschooler to know God?

9. Pray for each child in your care. Pray that God will use you as an example of His love.

About the Writer

Joye Smith is ministry consultant for children and preschoolers for Woman's Missionary Union®, Birmingham, Alabama.

Resources for Parents and Teachers

- Haystead, Wes. 1974. *Teaching Your Child About God.* Ventura, CA: Regal Books.

- Gillespie, V. Bailey. 1988. *The Experience of Faith.* Birmingham, AL: Religious Education Press.

- Mahand, Melinda and Clara Mae Van Brink. 1996. *Love, Laughter, & Learning.* Nashville, TN: Convention Press.

- Osborne, Rick. 1997. *Teaching Your Child How to Pray.* Chicago, IL: Moody Press.

- Powers, Bruce P. 1982. *Growing Faith.* Nashville, TN: Broadman Press.

- Reeves, Rhonda R. 1997. *200+ Ways to Care for Preschoolers.* Birmingham, AL: New Hope.

- Shelly Judith Allen. 1982. *The Spiritual Needs of Children.* Downers Grove, IL: InterVarsity Press.

- Waldrop, C. Sybil. 1985. *Guiding Your Child Toward God.* Nashville, TN: Broadman Press.

- Wright, H. Norman and Gary J. Oliver. 1999. *Raising Kids to Love Jesus.* Ventura, CA: Regal Books.

Notes

[1] All Scripture references from the Holy Bible, New International Version. Copyright © 1973, 1978, 1984 International Bible Society. Used by permission of Zondervan Bible Publishers.

[2] V. Bailey Gillespie, *The Experience of Faith* (Birmingham, AL: Religious Education Press, 1988), 91.

[3] Bruce Powers, *Growing Faith* (Nashville, TN: Broadman Press, 1982), 15.

[4] Gillespie, *The Experience of Faith*, 90.

[5] H. Norman Wright and Gary J. Oliver, *Raising Kids to Love Jesus* (Ventura, CA: Regal Books, 1999), 38.

[6] Powers, *Growing Faith*, 143.

[7] Denise George, *Kids Can Talk to God* (Birmingham, AL: New Hope Publishers, 1999), 20.

[8] Gillespie, *The Experience of Faith*, 94.

Chapter 2

Appropriate Learning for Young Children

by Sue Bredekamp

P arents, teachers, extended family, and community members—virtually all adults who care about young children
today—share a concern about the stresses in our society
that affect young children's development. These tough issues
include violence, drug abuse, disease, family issues, and special
needs, some of which are addressed more specifically in other
chapters of this book. Other issues arise unexpectedly as the
pace of change in our society continues to increase and the media become more and more intrusive in our family lives. Only
a few examples are needed to convey the enormous pressure experienced by children, parents, and teachers:

• A government office building, housing a child-care center,
  is bombed in Oklahoma City killing 162 innocent people,

including many children.

- The television carries images of American bombs falling on Kosovo and reports of children or their parents as victims.
- Government officials constantly accuse each other of lying, undermining public trust, and confusing young people.
- The powerful images of the media regularly expose young children to role models of unacceptable behavior, making it very difficult for adults to protect children and to teach them appropriate alternatives.

In fact, the idea that childhood is a special time of life in need of protection from adult views and experiences is seriously threatened if not all but lost today. Given such conditions, which any one parent or teacher cannot begin to change, what should concerned adults do? Solving society's problems is not the responsibility of young children. It is the responsibility of adults to protect children from potentially harmful experiences to the degree possible. Toward this goal, children need regular, consistent reminders that grown-ups, whether at home, school, child care, or church, love them and will do everything in their power to take care of them. At the same time, adults have a responsibility to help children develop emotionally, socially, cognitively, and morally so that they can develop the skills they will need to cope with the complexities of their current experiences and to solve social problems in the future.

The premise of this chapter is that the most effective intervention strategy, and one that applies to all the situations described above, as well as those articulated in other chapters, is for adults, drawing on what is known about how young children learn most effectively, to teach and support young children's optimal learning and development in all areas—physical, emotional, social, intellectual, and spiritual. The idea is to equip young children with the skills they need to function in an ever-changing, unpredictable world. To achieve this goal, adults must first understand how children develop and learn so they can apply that knowledge in helping children develop to their full potential.

Principles of Child Development and Learning

Children develop and learn best in the context of a community where they are safe and valued, their physical needs are met, and they feel psychologically secure.

We start with the most basic principle to emphasize the adults' responsibility in protecting children from harm and providing a secure base from which to explore the world. Research shows that even in the most stressful, violent circumstances, children are more likely to become resilient and successful if they have had a loving, nurturing relationship with at least one adult (preferably many more), most often a parent, but sometimes extended family members or teachers.[1] In programs for young children, this principle translates into the need to provide as much continuity as possible in the relationships between the adult caregivers and very young children. The "community" that provides this nurturing support can be the child's actual neighborhood, but it can also be their child-care program, school, or church, as long as there are consistent adults who know the child and family and communicate with them over time.

The foundation of all human development and learning is in the ability to establish and maintain a limited number of primary relationships with adults and other children.[2] These primary relationships begin in the family but extend over time to include teachers and other members of the community. This principle is especially important when we consider the stressors that children are exposed to early in life. When children feel physically safe and psychologically secure, they are better able to cope with stress and change, make friends, and learn.

Another application of this principle is that children need organized, predictable environments in which to live and learn. If the environment is safe and healthy, but also includes interesting, achievable but challenging learning experiences and materials, children's development and learning will be enhanced. To support the development of social competence, children need opportunities to make choices and learn decision-making within an organized environment. Early childhood classrooms should be structured so that young children have a variety of meaningful choices; they may play with blocks or clay, dress up, paint, read books, write, or draw. And they need to experience the consequences of their choices; for example, the adult will say things like, "You stayed too long in the block area today so you won't have time to paint." "If you choose to throw the sand, you have to leave the sand table until tomorrow when you can try again." These kind of small, seemingly inconsequential decisions add up to the more difficult tasks of decision-making that children will face later.

Ways of teaching children need to be developmentally appropriate, that is, they need to vary with the age, experience, and ability of the individual learners.

Looking across the early years of life from birth through age 8, a great deal of growth, development, and change takes place. Some things are generally to be expected of children at different ages and stages of development and that information can be used to plan experiences or curriculum so that they are safe, healthy, interesting, and achievable, but also challenging for children.[3] Parents and teachers must ask, "What are preschoolers typically like and how do they learn?" Based on this information, adults can select and/or adapt materials and activities for individuals and groups of children. For instance, storybook reading is a very useful teaching strategy for all ages, but the level and kind of book, as well as how it is used, will vary a great deal with the age of the learners. For example, preschoolers can listen in small groups and talk about the story, although they aren't very good at listening to each other. They are also more likely to engage with a book that has images or characters that look like them and with whom they can identify.

Storybook reading is an especially valuable strategy for dealing with tough issues today because many fine books, appropriate for various ages, are now available. Children's librarians are excellent resources for helping identify age-appropriate books. Nevertheless, adults, whether teachers or parents, should read the book in advance to be sure they are comfortable with the author's treatment of the subject and they should give children plenty of opportunity to talk about what is read. Books on tough issues are also best read to individuals or very small groups of children. Similarly, while adults need to talk to children about stressful situations, they need to follow the child's cues. Sometimes, we give much more information than children want or need at the time, or we fail to answer their real question, because we don't listen first.

Just as a great deal of predictable variation in children's development exists, a great deal of individual variation exists because each child has a unique pattern and timing of growth and development, as well as individual personality, family background, language and culture, learning style, and experiences. So for a prepared curriculum or teaching plan to be developmentally appropriate, it must be not only age appropriate, but also individually and culturally appropriate as well (that is, relevant and meaningful to the particular group of children served by the program.) The issues faced in a community or by individual families will vary, so teachers and caregivers need to be especially sensitive and open to supporting children and their families as needed.

Areas of development and learning are integrated and interdependent. Development in one area—physical, social, emotional, cognitive, spiritual—influences and is influenced by development and learning in other areas.

Among early childhood educators, this principle is called, "The Whole Child." We see this principle in practice when a precocious toddler starts to walk early (physical development), which opens up a larger world and more people with whom to interact, which enhances the child's learning and social skills. By the same token, the late walker of the same age has less variety of experience, and is often talked to less often by adults and older children. It is an understanding of this principle that tends to make adults particularly concerned about the tough issues that children face today. We realize that emotional stressors like divorce, chronic illness, or violence can affect children's development in other areas, such as intellectually or socially. But fortunately, positive experiences in any area of life can mediate the negatives as well. So it is important that preschoolers have many opportunities to be successful, and not get discouraged by experiencing repeated failure or frustration. When children accumulate especially satisfying experiences, such as friendships or success in new skills like writing their names or riding a tricycle, they gain self-esteem, which in turn helps them to weather the tough times in other areas.

Children are active learners, constructing their own understanding through concrete experiences with objects and other people, including modeling the behavior of esteemed adults or older children and being guided in their behavior.

It is important for adults to understand that in general, young children do not think or learn the same way adults do. They are concrete learners, which means that they learn best from firsthand experience, either hands-on with objects or by interacting with or observing esteemed adults or other children. Children don't learn complex concepts, especially ideas about right and wrong, by coloring workbooks, marking correct answers on a ditto sheet, or listening to adult lectures. Children learn very effectively through modeling, almost too well; they are better at observing and modeling the behavior of significant adults or other children than they are at listening.

When preschoolers become aggressive, they are often acting out behavior they have seen on TV or on the playground. Modeling is so powerful because aggression is very visible. More positive solutions are less visible, so adults need to help children see alternatives and sometimes, directly coach them.[4] If adults treat children with respect, for example, they are much more likely to get respectful replies than if they demand them in harsh, punishing tones. Similarly, children learn to share when generous adults share with them and praise them for their generosity.

Children need a concrete experience to help understand something new the same way adults need a concrete example to make a new idea meaningful. Young children are literal people. They are constantly trying to make sense of the world around them and they usually relate something new to something they already know. This is part of what makes them so much fun to be around and why they say so many funny, charming things. When Katelyn was four years old, her aunt saw her in swimming goggles and remarked, "Katelyn, you look so *official* in your goggles." Katelyn replied smartly, "I'm not a *fish*. I'm a kid." Every parent has observed the literal thinking of young children. During a Thanksgiving party at child care, Zoey learned that Indians used to live here. She went home that night and reported to her mother that Indians used to live in their apartment. No doubt she assumed that they were the previous tenants.

Because children don't think like adults, we often underestimate their thinking powers and sometimes assume incorrectly they are unaware of the stressors in their environment or the negative messages the media conveys. The fact that children do not yet think like adults (and won't until adolescence) must guide our work with them on tough issues. It means that we have to take time to listen to them to see what they really understand. Often, we will be surprised about what they really think. Because they may not have the language to describe their understanding, we must also use concrete, hands-on experiences to help them learn about the world and to express their understanding of it. We can gain great insight into children's feelings and fears by observing their play and art.

Play is an important vehicle for young children's social, emotional, and cognitive development as well as a context for development.

James Garbarino and his colleagues have studied the effects on young children growing up in war zones like Northern Ireland and Vietnam, as well as children whose life experience is similarly stressful in highly violent communities in the United States. He has found that several factors are important to help these children become psychologically healthy. Among those factors are consistency of adult relationships, organized and predictable environments (both of which have been addressed under the first principle), and opportunities to express feelings through play and art.[5]

For very young children, play is not only the best context for their learning and development to occur, but it is also the best context for adults to observe or interact with children so as to learn what they understand and are able to do. In play, children "stand head and shoulders above" what they normally do. They can conquer their fears of monsters or bad guys, or learn to control their aggressive impulses by acting out a role. They can also practice roles of helping adults like police, firefighters, parents, or teachers. But even knowing the value of play, adults cannot just assume that children will play productively. One kindergarten teacher set up a store in her class for children to play and learn about economics and literacy. Unfortunately, the children in this disadvantaged neighborhood continually played robbing the store. Their own experience was insufficient to result in productive play. Instead of simply removing the props, the teacher established a relationship with a local grocery to which the children made regular visits. Then back at school, she herself entered the pretend store as a "customer" and modeled purchasing groceries, asking prices, and demonstrating the "script" of behavior that people use in stores. Soon she saw more productive, valuable play that increased children's vocabularies and their literacy and math skills (making grocery lists, recognizing print on cereal boxes, comparing prices, counting change, etc.) But equally important, she taught them an acceptable alternative to behavior they were modeling and practicing.

Children's art work is a wonderful way to gain insight into their thinking about tough issues and what they understand. Children will often express their feelings through painting or drawing. Adults can engage in conversation about the picture or the painting, which is a safer way of talking than directly confronting a negative experience the child has had. Children's words can be captured on audiotape or through dictation so the adult can reflect on them later, or compare them to future art projects and expressions to see change.

Early experience has both cumulative and delayed effects on in-dividual children's development; there are optimal periods for certain types of development.

The principle of cumulative effects is very important in re-lation to tackling the tough issues that face parents and chil-dren today. What this means is relatively simple—the more exposure to stress that children receive the more likely they are to suffer deleterious effects. For example, watching violent tele-vision programming occasionally most certainly does not cre-ate violent offenders. But a steady diet of exposure to violent media has been found to desensitize children to the suffering and feelings of others.[6] If that exposure occurs in a context where real-life experiences of violence occur, such as commu-nity or domestic violence, then the cumulative effect can be serious.

At the same time, we know that trauma in early childhood can have delayed effects. A child who is abused may not show evi-dence of negative effects at the time, but the damage becomes evident years later. Because of the potential for delayed effects, adults must remain consistently nurturing, supportive, and available.

Also related to this principle is the idea that there are opti-mal times for development to occur. For instance, the early years of life are clearly the time when language development occurs rapidly. We now know that the language that children hear and the way adults talk with children during the first three years of life lay an important foundation for brain development and for all later learning.[7] When children hear encouraging, positive messages during those early years, they in turn will produce more language and will be more likely to initiate positive conversations at age four. What's required isn't difficult— it's the "motherese" type talk when a toddler points to the refrigerator and the parent supplies the words, "would you like some juice?" or when the child tries to explore the environment, adults are encouraging and provide opportunities including real-life objects like keys or pots and pans. Unfortunately, some children grow up in homes where little conversation is directed at them, all talk is brief and directive (Go to bed, be quiet), and where their initiatives are discouraged or punished. In cases such as these, the preschool teacher has greater responsibility to provide many opportunities for children to talk with more capable speakers as well as lots of fun and interesting things to talk about.

A final example of cumulative effects and optimal periods is the development of social interactions. Throughout early childhood, young children are slowly acquiring the ability to move from focusing solely on themselves and their own needs to relating to other people and making friends. This developmental process takes time and depends on many other developments, such as adequate language and reaching a level of intellectual development where they understand another person's point of view. But it is a vitally important process because we know that children who are unable to make friends, are neglected, or are rejected by their peers at age six or seven, are more likely to have difficulty in school, to eventually drop out, less likely to marry and hold productive employment, and to be at risk for other antisocial outcomes.[8] During the preschool years, we can see children who have difficulty making friends and are rejected by other children. We know that if adults intervene during those early years and coach children in ways to relate to others and how to make friends, this cycle can be reversed early.

Application and Reflection

The six principles are presented here to provide basic guidance for teachers and parents when they confront tough issues that young children encounter today. No simple solutions to help young children and families cope with stress exist. But these principles, based on what is generally known about preschool children, can help guide our decisions about what strategies are likely to be most helpful.

Let's return to some of the examples of the kinds of tough issues listed at the outset that adults must help children deal with. In light of the principles, reflect on these situations:

1. What do you do when children are exposed to violent or tragic content via the media?
Don't assume they are unaware of events in the world. Listen carefully to their conversation and observe their play to see what they may be thinking about. Know that we can never reassure them enough that the responsible adults in their lives are doing everything possible to keep them safe.

2. What can you do if children are more directly affected by violence or other tough issues?
Be sure that children have consistent, loving adults to help them feel safe and secure. Provide orderly, predictable environments in which to play and learn. Give them many opportunities to express their feelings through their play and art, and in conversation.

3. What can you do when children get mixed messages about right and wrong through the media or in their experiences?

Watch television with children and talk to them about what they see so that they can learn to be critical thinkers about what is presented in the media.[9] Talk to children about what they understand. Don't expect them to understand morality the way adults do, but tell them what you think in simple language— "Sometimes people do bad things, like tell lies. But God wants us to tell the truth." If something uncomfortable is presented, initiate the conversation by expressing an opinion, "I don't like this show. I don't like to see people getting hurt. Let's watch something else."

4. What can you do if a child is struggling with a tough issue and it is clearly affecting his behavior at home and in preschool?
Parents and other caregivers or teachers need to stay in close communication about what happens in children's lives. They don't have to agree on everything but they do need to problem-solve together how best to respond to children's anxieties and fears. If a child is withdrawn or aggressive, for instance, and that behavior is affecting his ability to make friends or enjoy preschool, parents and teachers need to support each other in strategies to help the child.[10] Maybe, all that's needed is allowing a special, highly desirable toy to be brought to preschool to share with other children, or another child can be invited over for lunch. Perhaps a more directive approach may be required. Making friends isn't automatic, but not making friends has lasting negative consequences. Supportive relationships are vital protection against tough times, and resilient children, the kind who know how to make friends, are able to tackle the tough issues that life inevitably presents.

Conclusion

The principles and their application can be illustrated through an example. On the morning of March 31, 1981, I found myself observing in a class of four- and five-year-olds. The morning began with Show and Tell, mostly Tell in this instance. The morning was unusual, however, because the preceding afternoon an assassination attempt had been made on the life of President Reagan. That morning there was still a great deal of uncertainty as to the prognosis of the President and the three other men wounded in the shooting. Not surprisingly, the assassination attempt was the prime topic for "telling" that morning. With a cool detachment that Dan Rather would have envied, one child after another stood and calmly and accurately related the events of the shooting. "The bullet entered the left lobe of his lung." "Mr. Brady was shot over his left eye and the bullet passed through the right side of his brain." At least 10 children "shared" various aspects of the shooting incident. The teacher's only response was to repeatedly say, "The President is feeling better now." Following the allotted 20 minutes of Show and Tell, the teacher proceeded to the lesson of the day, which concerned the letter Q.

How could that morning have been different? The curriculum and teaching strategies could have been more developmentally appropriate—that is, more responsive to the age and individual variation of the children. Time spent squirming during Show and Tell could have been spent in child-initiated activities, among which would have been dramatic play where children could express strong feelings such as their fear and concern about the news. They might have acted out their TV anchor-selves, which would have helped them feel some control in the situation. Children would also have had an opportunity to dictate stories or use a computer to write them. Children would definitely have had a chance to express their feelings in art work. Parents would have been able to see the stories and pictures and follow up with their children, discussing their own concerns about the situation. All of these opportunities for important social, emotional, cognitive, and moral development were missed.

Fortunately, presidential assassination attempts are rare events in children's lives, but every day brings something different that may be comparably stressful. No quick fix or bandage will suffice. Parents, teachers, and other concerned adults need to work together to support preschool children's healthy development and learning.

About the Writer

Sue Bredekamp, Ph.D., works for the Council for Early Childhood Professional Recognition. She has served on the staff of the National Association for the Education of Young Children and led in the study of developmentally appropriate practice there.

Resource

- J.M. Farish, "When Disaster Strikes: Helping Young Children Cope," National Association for the Education of Young Children leaflet #533. Available at www.naeyc.org.

Notes

[1]National Association for the Education of Young Children, Position statement on violence in the lives of children, *Young Children*, 48, no. 6, 1993, 80–84; J. Garbarino, N. Dubrow, K. Kostelny, and C. Pardo,. *Children in danger: Coping with the consequences of community violence* (San Francisco: Jossey-Bass Publishers, 1992), 47, 55.

[2]Carnegie Task Force on Meeting the Needs of Young Children, *Starting Points: Meeting the Needs of Our Youngest Children* (New York: Carnegie Corporation, 1994), 9, 12.

[3]S. Bredekamp, and C. Copple, (Eds.), *Developmentally appropriate practice in early childhood programs*. Rev. ed. (Washington, DC: National Association for the Education of Young Children, 1997), 9–15.

[4]R. G. Slabey, W. C. Roedell, D. Arezzo, and K. Hendrix, *Early violence prevention: Tools for teachers of young children* (Washington, DC: National Association for the Education of Young Children, 1995), 108, 121, 155–161.

[5]Garbarino and others, *Children in danger*, 202, 221.

[6]National Association for the Education of Young Children, Position statement on media violence in children's lives. *Young Children*, 45, no. 5, 1990, 18–21

[7]T. Hart, and B. Risley, *Meaningful differences in the everyday experience of young American children* (Baltimore: Paul H. Brookes Publishing, 1995), 132.

[8]S. Asher, P. Renshaw, and S. Hymel,. "Peer relations and the development of social skills," in S. Moore & C. Cooper (Eds.), *The young child: Reviews*

of research, 3, (Washington, DC: National Association for the Education of Young Children, 1982), 137–158;. L. Katz, and D. McClellan, *Fostering children's social competence: The teacher's role* (Washington, DC: National Association for the Education of Young Children, 1997), 17–19.

[9]National Association for the Education of Young Children, Position statement on media violence in children's lives, 18–21.

[10]R. G. Slabey, and others. *Early violence prevention*, 179–180.

Chapter 3

Helping Young Children Deal with Family Violence

by Donna S. Quick, Darla Botkin, and Sam Quick

Every day thousands of young children experience family violence, either as direct victims of brutality or as observers of violence to family members. According to a family violence expert, "In our society, people are more likely to be killed and physically assaulted, abused and neglected, and sexually assaulted and molested in their own homes and by other family members than anywhere else or by anyone else" (Gelles, 1994, p. 262).

Teachers of young children need to be aware of the types of family violence, their prevalence, the common effects of family violence on young children, and ways that caring adults can help.

Types and Prevalence of Family Violence

Several different types of family violence, and the family relationships involved, have been defined (see pages 61–62). Any child who lives in an environment where one or more of these forms of abuse occurs, whether he or she is the direct victim or an observer of the abuse, will suffer detrimental effects (McCloskey, Figueredo, & Koss, 1995).

The prevalence of these forms of abuse among American families is staggering. Anyone who teaches young children is likely to have one or more children in the class who are experiencing some form of family violence.

Among the best sources of information about the prevalence of family violence are the two National Family Violence Surveys which were done in 1975 and 1985 (Gelles & Straus, 1987, 1988; Straus & Gelles, 1986; Straus, Gelles, & Steinmetz, 1980). These surveys were conducted using phone interviews with an anonymous adult member of the family and drew on nationally representative samples (Gelles, 1994). These studies revealed that each year, 1.5 million children are victims of parental physical violence and 450,000 children are injured as a result of parental violence.

Findings from many other studies are summarized here:

- An estimated 6 to 62 percent of female children and 3 to 31 percent of male children are victims of sexual abuse (Peters, Wyatt, & Finkelhor, 1986).
- Some 1,300 children are killed by their parents or caretakers each year (Daro, 1992).

- Based on families' self-reported data, children in 16 percent of homes in the United States experience violence between their parents each year (Gelles & Straus, 1988; Straus & Gelles, 1986). More than one-fourth of the adults surveyed reported that some form of marital violence had occurred at least once during the course of their marriage.
- On average, a woman who is a victim of spouse or partner abuse will be abused three times a year, indicating her children will probably observe and be affected by these violent acts just as frequently (Johnson, 1995.)
- Homicide between intimate adults accounts for between 20 to 40 percent of all murders in the United States (Curtis, 1974).
- Each year, 680 husbands and boyfriends are killed by their wives and girlfriends, while 1,300 wives and girlfriends are killed by their husbands and boyfriends (US Department of Justice, 1991). As part of the tragic aftermath of these incidents, the children of these adults are traumatized and suffer long-term pain, fear, and confusion (Wolfe, Zak, Jaffe, & Wilson, 1986).

What sense can children make of the two persons they love the most striking out at each other with such ferocity that death is not an uncommon result?

Only in the last two decades has elder abuse been recognized as a serious problem. A study of 2,020 noninstitutionalized elderly persons found that 32 individuals per 1,000 reported experiencing physical violence, verbal aggression, and/or neglect in the past year (Pillemer & Finkelhor, 1988). Twenty older persons per 1,000 experienced physical violence. Spouses were found to be the most frequent abusers, with an equal amount of men and women as victims. How many grandchildren and great-grandchildren are exposed to this violence, and what are they learning about the care of elderly loved ones?

Although violence among siblings in the United States is one of the most frequent forms of family violence, the issue continues to be neglected by family members and professionals (Gelles, 1995). "Children will be children" seems to be the prevailing attitude, implying it is natural for children to abuse each other. The National Family Violence Surveys found that 109,000 children used guns or knives in fights with siblings in the year before the survey was conducted (Straus, Gelles, & Steinmetz, 1980). Although this type of behavior toward a nonfamily member would not be tolerated, it is often ignored when it occurs between children in a family system.

Finally, the most recent form of family violence to receive attention is that of child-to-parent violence. This has been sensationalized in the media by a few highly publicized cases of children being charged with murdering their wealthy parents, and yet there continues to be much denial about the actual frequency of parental abuse. The National Family Violence Surveys found that approximately 75,000 to 1 million parents experience violent acts against them by their teenage children each year (Cornell & Gelles, 1982). If there are young children in some of these homes, how terrified they must be to see the person who is to protect them, their parent, being beaten by an older sibling.

Society's increasing acknowledgment of the existence and prevalence of family violence has led to concern about the effects of family violence on young children (Gelles, 1993). How does growing up in a violent home affect children's development and behavior? How can teachers (relatives, adult friends, and caregivers) of young children identify and help these children?

Types of Family Violence

Family violence may be broadly defined as any form of physical, verbal, emotional, or psychological maltreatment between or among two or more family members (Gelles, 1995). The family members need not be biologically related. Any person who is defined as a member of a family system may be a perpetrator or a victim. For example, a mother's cohabiting boyfriend who physically abuses her biological son would be defined as a perpetrator of family violence. Likewise, a nonresidential grandmother who beats her grandchildren when she baby-sits is committing family violence.

Physical violence includes all forms of physically violent acts against another person such as hitting, kicking, pulling hair, burning with a cigarette, or tying someone to a chair or bed (Straus, 1991). Most definitions of physical abuse also include sexual molestation and mistreatment.

Child sexual abuse can range from an adult exposing himself or herself to a young child, to sexual intercourse between the child and the perpetrator (Finkelhor, 1979, 1984).

Emotional/psychological abuse includes acts such as placing unrealistic demands on a family member, not allowing another to have a separate sense of self or autonomy, and denying normal developmental progression. Any behavior that intimidates or terrorizes another would be a form of emotional/psychological abuse (Gil, 1996).

Verbal abuse includes calling another demeaning and hurtful names, unnecessary criticism, and excessive yelling or raging (Gil, 1996).

Neglect is defined as acts that deprive another of adequate food, shelter, medical care, or developmentally appropriate supervision (Gil, 1996).

Family violence can also be defined by the relationships of family members involved. The abuse can be *adult to child* (i.e. physical child abuse, sexual child abuse), *adult to adult* (i.e. spouse or partner abuse, elder abuse), *child to child* (i.e., sibling abuse, cousin abuse), or *child to parent* (parental abuse) (Gelles, 1995).

Effects of Family Violence on Children

Studies have shown time and time again that violence in the lives of children can have devastating effects on their social, emotional, and/or cognitive development (Garbarino, Dubrow, Kosteiny, & Pardo, 1992; Johnson, 1989; Terr, 1990). Beyond frequent physical harm, specific reactions by children may include fear, worry, doubt, and confusion.

In addition, chronic exposure to family violence can have serious developmental consequences for children including psychological disorders, grief and loss reactions, impaired intellectual development, school problems, truncated moral development, pathological adaptation to violence, identification with the aggressor, and difficulty focusing on school work (Craig, 1992; Garbarino, Dubor, Kosteiny, & Pardo, 1992).

Watching and listening to abusive family members leaves emotional scars (Henderson, 1995). These include low self-esteem, mixed feelings toward adults in the family, lack of trust, anxiety associated with anticipating the next outbreak of violence, guilt and depression due to feeling responsible for the abuse, and fear of abandonment. Children who are abused may fail to thrive physically or may have speech and hearing problems. They often suffer from stress-related illness such as headaches and stomachaches (Osofsky, 1995).

Children in violent homes may be aggressive or extremely passive (Wolfner & Gelles, 1992). Girls frequently assume a maternal role in caring for the other children. A boy may take on the role of the father as the mother becomes more dependent on him. Children often experience problems in school (e.g., failing grades, truancy, and dropping out). There is a higher rate of juvenile delinquency and substance abuse among these youth. Teenagers often escape violent homes into early marriages or pregnancies. In addition, children from violent homes may suffer post-traumatic stress, resulting from feelings of being overwhelmed and helpless (Gondolf, 1989).

Indicators of Abuse and Neglect

The following characteristics are often associated with higher incidences of abuse: poverty, blue-collar employment, unemployment, families with two or more children, parents who were victims of abuse, families going through stressful change (moving, health problems, marital difficulties, or work changes), and families which are more punitive and less empathic (Germain, Brassard, Hart, 1985). When these factors are present and abuse is suspected, children should be considered to be at greater risk. Note: Families in these situations may be at higher risk, but abuse occurs across all socio-economic lines.

Various characteristics are associated with family violence and neglect (see below). While these signs may indicate other problems, they can help determine if abuse or neglect is occurring.

Signs of Possible Abuse

Child-related signs
- Suspicious burns, bruises, injuries
- Often tired, hungry, or dirty
- Inadequate dental or medical care
- Extreme aggression or passivity
- Major developmental lags
- Afraid of family members or other adults
- Unpleasant or demanding behavior
- Often does not obey
- Mood swings
- Unusually shy—avoids other children and adults
- Avoids physical contact

- Apt to seek affection from any adult
- Child reports being hurt or abused
- Unusual sexual awareness or behavior

Family member or caregiver signs
- Misuse of alcohol or other drugs
- Disorganized, upset home life
- Does not seem to care what happens
- Isolated, doesn't get along with others
- Uses inappropriate, harsh discipline
- Seems unconcerned about child
- Sees child as very bad or evil
- Questionable explanation of injury to child

Factors that Protect Against Family Violence

A literature review of risk factors (Smith, Williams & Rosen, 1990) suggests that the following protective factors may decrease the probability of violence in families:
- a strong social network of friends and extended family
- no past history of violence in one's family of origin
- available resources (financial, educational, health, and psychological)
- community support
- use of various coping mechanisms (e.g., talking about feelings or healthy physical activity)
- no chemical dependencies
- ability to manage unpredictable stressors
- high levels of family cohesion and adaptability

Suggestions for Helping Children

The Best Approach: Prevention

The effects of family violence are far reaching and long lasting (Emde, 1993). Throughout their lives, children are likely to suffer the consequences of emotional and physical damage from abuse. Some children die. Many grow up to become abusive adults. Society pays a high price in violence, legal fees, lost creativity, and expensive social service programs.

Prevention programs work, and they cost far less than the social and economic price paid after abuse has happened (Hampton, Gullotta, Adams, Potter, & Weissberg, 1993). Successful preventive programs include:

- prenatal support and education
- education on parenting for family members
- accessible, high-quality child care
- early health care and developmental screening
- stress-management skills and impulse control
- self-help groups, including family support groups
- home health visitors and foster grandparents
- religious and community programs

Create a Nurturing Classroom Climate

Schools and child-care programs play a major role in the socialization of children. Teachers of young children can create a classroom climate that conveys a sense of safety and encourages nonviolent ways to manage conflict (Levin, 1994; Carlsson-Paige & Levin, 1985).

According to the National Association for the Education of Young Children (NAEYC), "Practices that lead to high-quality programs help reduce the likelihood of abuse of children in out-of-home settings, and high-quality programs can provide support to families to reduce instances of abuse in the home," (NAEYC Position Statement on Prevention of Child Abuse, 1997, p. 46).

The following suggestions, in keeping with high-quality early childhood programs, create a classroom environment that helps to prevent, reduce, and heal abusive behavior.

Reassure children that they are safe. All adults in the program (bus drivers, cooks, teachers) let children know that they are loved and that the adults will do their very best to take care of all the children. Adults who sense children's needs are encouraged to be extra generous with hugs and other expressions of warmth and affection.

Provide opportunities for children to express their feelings. In the wake of violence, children experience a range of feelings including fear, worry, doubt, confusion, sadness, anger, and guilt. By words and through example, show children that their feelings are important. Teachers can usually encourage very young children to show their feelings more effectively through activities (e.g., drawing, puppet play, role play) rather than by trying to get them to talk directly about their feelings (Wallach, 1995). Provide opportunities for these types of activities as a regular part of the program, thoughtfully observe children as they play, and follow up with children who convey messages that they may have experienced some type of violence and are having difficulties.

Be honest and realistic. Early childhood professionals cannot guarantee that violence will not strike the children in their care. It is important to be honest about the inevitability of conflict in everyone's life. Strive to find a balance between helping a child feel safe and acknowledging the existence of conflict. Do this in a manner appropriate to the child's ability to understand, emphasizing reassurance.

Model calmness and control. Children react intuitively to the feelings of family members, caregivers, and teachers. Even very young children pick up on adults' uncertainty, helplessness, sadness, and anger. Professionals cannot hide feelings, but can rise to the occasion and exercise an innate sense of mastery. Bring forth inner calm, courage, and strength in helping children manage conflict in the classroom and in their homes.

Create a classroom constitution. Help children set up guidelines for preventing and managing conflict. Keep the rules short, simple, and positive about what to do. Talk, live, and apply these rules until they become second nature for the children. For example, many teachers use the following three rules: 1) We are kind to each other. 2) We listen to feelings. 3) We use words to solve problems.

Refuse to tolerate abusive behavior among children. When conflict among children suddenly escalates into meanness, name calling, or hitting, gently stop the behavior. Model calmness and explain that intentionally hurting one another is not allowed. "People are not for hitting or calling names. Use your words to talk about feelings and solve problems." Addressing the issue of violent behavior by children toward children is of paramount importance. The Peace Education Foundation (see resources) offers excellent resources to encourage peaceful resolution of differences among children.

Encourage strength and sensitivity in all children. A proactive commitment on the part of the school staff to reduce sexual stereotyping (i.e., not encouraging aggressive dominant behavior in male children and passive/submissive behavior in female children) can be an important factor in reducing the prevalence of family violence.

Teach problem-solving skills. When conflict situations arise in the classroom, use them to teach children steps for solving problems peacefully. With very young children, use a simple process such as: 1) Name the problem. 2) Talk about ways to help. 3) Try a solution.

For older children, a process such as the following may be appropriate: 1) Children identify the problem and reach consensus on the issue so that everyone is invested in finding a solution. 2) Children brainstorm as many solutions to the problem as they can discover. 3) Children explore the consequences of all identified solutions. 4) Children choose a solution that everyone is willing to try. 5) Children implement the solution. 6) Children follow up to see if the solution is working (Slaby, Roedell, Arezzo & Hendrix, 1995).

Tune in to expressions of anger. Children who have witnessed or experienced violence may begin to imitate the role of the perpetrator or take on the role of the abuser, neither of which is in the children's best interests. Sometimes they release their emotional pressure in anger. Two exercises may be useful for teachers to understand children's anger and help them to express it. At a time of calm, have children who are often angry think of two things which make them angry. Discuss them together. Next, children identify things they do when they get angry. Analyze and discuss the list with them. Are these reactions appropriate? Support children by modeling, reading suitable children's books, and coaching children to find more positive ways to deal with their anger.

Encourage a sense of hope. Help children remain optimistic. Get across the message that most people are good, caring individuals who will do whatever they can to help each other out. Make it possible for children to get to know people within and beyond the school who exemplify this message. Find out about real-life heroes and heroines in children's books and in the media. In simple language, explain that each of us has an important part to play in creating a world that is safe, a world that brings out the best in each of us, a world where love and creative solutions flourish (McMath, 1997).

Scatter kindness. Counter violence with kindness. Help children daily to identify ways in which they can express kindness among themselves and to others. Encourage each child to perform one act of kindness each day (e.g., help a friend find his or her mittens or make a thank-you picture for the elderly woman who helps at snack time).

Beyond the Classroom

Know when to seek professional help. If a child shows continued distress or persistent signs of anxiety such as withdrawal, increased aggression, nightmares, clinging, headaches, tummy aches, shyness, poor concentration, or sleep/appetite changes, consider an evaluation by a mental health professional who specializes in caring for children.

Let a strong voice be heard. Teachers of young children have power; early educators can make a difference! Become an advocate for public policies and programs which protect and nurture children of all ages. In the local community, and in each state and the nation, act to ensure that every child has a right to a safe, loving upbringing in a nonviolent and kind family and community. Offer staff training about the dynamics and prevention of family violence. Work with other professionals and know about resources in the community (Miller, 1996).

When a Child Discloses Abuse

The Role of Early Childhood Professionals

Because teachers have a unique relationship with the children in their classrooms, and because young children typically hold them in high esteem, children often will feel safe enough to disclose abusive situations to their teachers. When this happens, keep the following guidelines in mind:

- Believe the child.
- Try to stay calm.
- Reassure and support the child; for example, say, "I appreciate that you told me. You did the right thing."

- Take time to respond to the child's questions and concerns.
- When the developmental level of the child warrants, tell the child what will be done with the information and that by law teachers must report the abuse.
- Explain what will happen next.
- Inform the director or other superior immediately, in accordance with program or school policy and state law.
- Continue to stay with and support the child during the reporting period.
- Remain available to the child if he or she wants to talk about what has happened.
- Let the child know he or she did not cause the violence.
- Perhaps most importantly, teachers and caregivers need to give the child the opportunity to talk about what has happened in a nonthreatening environment. Many children cannot talk directly about what has happened, so provide activities to help children express their feelings: dramatic play, art activities, storytelling, and puppet play. Let the child take the lead and do not try to direct the play. Reflect back to the children their feelings and let them know their feelings are respected.

For further suggestions on helping children cope with family violence, see Wallach (1993) and Miller (1996) (found in reference section).

Further Suggestions

There are many ways to become actively involved in the prevention, reduction, and treatment of family violence:

- **Take a look at oneself.** Family members and child caregivers are urged to reach out for help if they feel overwhelmed.

- **Become better educated about parenthood.** It's one of the most important roles people ever play.

- **Look around with sensitive eyes, ears, and heart.** Learn the indicators of abuse and neglect. Be aware of what is going on. Report suspected abuse. If someone needs help with the stress of parenting, reach out.

- **Nurture and encourage children.** Express love and appreciation. Don't be too busy to give children a hug and a smile. A few words of encouragement and some moments of undivided attention make a big difference.

- **Get involved.** Start a family support group in the neighborhood. Request speakers on parenting for school or religious group meetings. Volunteer time or contribute financially.

- **Support neighbors and family members.** Prevention begins right in one's own home and neighborhood.

- **Don't overlook cruel behavior.** Society pays a high price when abuse goes unrecognized and uncorrected. Many adult survivors have low self-esteem and difficulties in relationships. They continue to blame themselves for being victimized. They stay angry toward the perpetrator. The roots of sexual dysfunction, eating disorders, alcoholism, and drug problems often lie in abusive backgrounds.

Application and Reflection

1. Define each type of family violence.

• Family violence

• Physical violence

• Child sexual abuse

• Emotional/psychological abuse

• Verbal abuse

• Neglect

2. What effects can family violence have on children?

3. How can you help children and families with young children who are exposed to violence?

4. How can you become actively involved to help families exposed to violence?

5. What are some signs of possible abuse or neglect?

Reflect on what God would have you do to help families living in violence. Spend time praying for anyone you may know who is involved in violent situations. Ask God to show you how you can help. **Write your prayer below:**

About the Writers

Donna S. Quick, Ph.D., is Associate Professor; Darla Botkin, Ph.D, is Associate Professor; and Sam Quick, Ph.D., is Extension Professor at the University of Kentucky, Department of Family Studies, College of Human Environmental Sciences, Lexington.

Reprinted by permission from *Dimensions of Early Childhood*, Winter 1999, published by Southern Early Childhood Association.

Selected Resources on Family Violence

- Parents Anonymous (PA) is a self-help program designed to help families prevent damaging relationships between themselves and their children. It is the largest national child abuse prevention and treatment program. PA offers a variety of resources. To find out about local PA groups, call the national office in California at (909) 621-6184 or visit on the Web at www.parentsanonymous.org.

- State laws require early childhood professionals who know about a case of family violence to report it. Each program for young children has policies and procedures for handling these situations. These might include calling the National

Domestic Violence Hotline at (800) 799-7233, the local police department, or another designated local or state agency.

- *I Told My Secret* is a pamphlet written for children ages 6 to 12 who have been abused. It answers pressing questions such as: "Will I ever forget?"; "Why did it happen?" and "Why do I have to see a therapist?" It can be read to children by their families, therapists, or teachers, and is available through Launch Press, (800) 321-9167.

- Peace Education Foundation, 1900 Biscayne Boulevard, Miami, FL 33132, phone (800) 749-8839. Publishers of *Peacemaking Skills for Little Kids* and *Fighting Fair for Families*.

- The National Center for Violence Prevention, phone (800) 962-6662. Produces videos, software, books, and games.

- *Kelly Bear Positive Behavior Book* by Leah Davies (1996), published by Kelly Bear Press, Inc., 4295 County Road 12, Lafayette, AL 36862.

- *The Impact of Domestic Violence on Children.* A booklet published by the American Bar Association Service Center, 750 North Lake Shore Drive, Chicago, IL 60611. To order, call (800) 285-2221. Specify reference number 549-0248. Cost is $6.

- Videos: *Secret Wounds: Working with Observers of Domestic Violence* is specifically designed to address the counseling needs of 6- to 13-year-olds who have witnessed family violence. Send $95 plus $4 for shipping and handling charges to: Banerjee Associates, Department 74, 178 Tamarack Circle, Skillman, NJ 08558. *You're Hurting Me, Too! The Effects of Domestic Violence on Children*. Examines both the short- and long-term effects of domestic violence on children. For more information, call (800) 553-8336.

References

Carlsson-Paige, N., & Levin, D.E. (1985). *Helping young children understand peace, war, and the nuclear threat*. Washington, DC: National Association for the Education of Young Children.

Cornell, C.P., & Gelles, R.J. (1982). Adolescent to parent violence. *Urban Social Change Review*, 15, 8–14.

Craig, S. (1992). The educational needs of children living with violence. *Phi Delta Kappan*, 74(1), 67–71.

Curtis, L. (1974). *Criminal Violence: National patterns and behavior*. Lexington, KY: Lexington Books.

Daro, D. (1992). *Current trends in child abuse reporting and fatalities: NCPCA's 1991 Annual Fifty State Survey*. Chicago: National Committee to Prevent Child Abuse.

Emde, RN (1993). The horror! The horror! Reflections on our culture of violence and its implications for early development and morality. *Psychiatry*, 56, 119–123.

Finkelhor, D. (1979). *Sexually victimized children*. New York: Free Press.

Finkelhor, D. (1984). *Child sexual abuse: New theories and research*. New York: Free Press.

Garbarino, J., Dubrow, N., Kosteiny, K., & Pardo, C. (1992). *Children in danger: Coping with the effects of community violence*. San Francisco: Jossey-Bass.

Gelles, R.J. (1993). Through a sociological lens: Social structures and family violence. In R.J. Gelles & D.R. Loseke (Eds.), *Current controversies on family violence* (pp. 31–46). Thousand Oaks, CA: Sage.

Gelles, R.J. (1994). Family violence, abuse and neglect. In P. McKenry & S. Price (Eds.), *Families and change: Coping with stressful events* (pp. 262–280). Thousand Oaks, CA: Sage.

Gelles, R.J. (1995). *Contemporary families: A sociological view.* Thousand Oaks, CA: Sage.

Gelles, R.J., & Straus, M.S. (1987). Is violence towards children increasing? A comparison of 1975 and 1985 national survey rates. *Journal of Interpersonal Violence,* 2, 212–222.

Gelles, R.J., & Straus, M.S. (1988) *Intimate violence.* New York: Simon & Schuster.

Germaine, R., Brassard, M., & Hart, S. (1985) Crisis intervention for maltreated children. *School Psychology Review,* 14, 291–299.

Gil, E. (1996). *Systemic treatment of families who abuse.* San Francisco: Jossey-Bass.

Gondolf, E. (1989). *Man against woman.* Blue Ridge Summit, PA: McGraw-Hill.

Hampton, R.L., Gullotta, T.P., Adams, G.R., Potter, E.H., & Weissberg, R. (Eds.). (1993). *Family violence: Prevention and treatment.* Thousand Oaks, CA: Sage.

Henderson, R. (1995, January/February). Caught in the crossfire. *Common Boundary,* 28–35.

Johnson, K. (1989) *Trauma in the lives of children.* Alameda: Hunter House.

Johnson, M.P. (1995) Patriarchal terrorism and common couple violence: Two forms of violence against women. *Journal of Marriage and the Family,* 57, 283–294.

Levin, D. (1994). *Teaching young children in violent times: Building a peaceable classroom.* Cambridge, MA: Educators for Social Responsibility.

McCloskey, L.A., Figueredo, A.J., & Koss, M.P. (1995). The effects of systemic family violence on children's mental health. *Child Development,* 66, 1239–1261.

McMath, J.S. (1997). Young children, national tragedy, and picture books. *Young Children*, 52, 82–84.

Miller, K. (1996). *The crisis manual for early childhood teachers: How to handle really difficult problems*. Beltsville, MD: Gryphon House.

National Association for the Education of Young Children. (1997, March). National Association for the Education of Young Children, position statement on prevention of child abuse in early childhood programs and the responsibilities of early childhood professionals to prevent child abuse. *Young Children*, 52(3), 42–46.

Osofsky, J.D. (1995). The effects of exposure to violence on young children. *American Psychologist*, 50, 782–788.

Peters, S.D., Wyatt, G.E., & Finkelhor, D. (1986). Prevalence. In D. Finkelhor (Ed.), *A sourcebook on child sexual abuse* (pp. 15–59). Thousand Oaks, CA: Sage.

Pillemer, K., & Finkelhor, D. (1988). The prevention of elder abuse: A random sample survey. *The Gerontologist*, 28, 51–57.

Slaby, R.G., Roedell, W.C., Arezzo, D., & Hendrix, K. (1995). *Early violence prevention: Tools for teachers of young children*. Washington, DC: National Association for the Education of Young Children.

Smith, S., Williams, M., & Rosen, K. (1990). *Violence hits home: Comprehensive treatment approaches to domestic violence*. New York: Springer.

Straus, M.A. (1991) Physical violence in American families; Incidence, rates, causes, and trends. In D. Knudsen & J.L. Miller (Eds.), *Abuser and batterer: Social and legal responses to family violence* (pp. 17–34). New York: Aldine de Gruyter.

Straus, M.A., & Gelles, R.J. (1986). Societal change and change in family violence from 1975 to 1985 as revealed in two national surveys. *Journal of Marriage and the Family*, 48, 465–479.

Straus, M.A., Gelles, R.J., & Steinmetz, S.K. (1980). *Behind closed doors*. Garden City, NY: Doubleday.

Terr, L. (1990) *Too scared to cry*. New York: Basic Books.

United States Department of Justice. (1991) *Uniform crime reports for the United States,* 1991. Washington, DC: US Department of Justice, Federal Bureau of Investigation.

Wallach, L.B. (1993). Helping children cope with violence. *Young Children* 48(4), 4–11.

Wallach, L.B. (1995). Breaking the cycle of violence. *Children Today,* 23, 26–31.

Wolfe, D.A., Zak, L., Jaffe, P., & Wilson, S.K. (1986). *Children of battered women.* Thousand Oaks, CA: Sage.

Wolfner, G.D. & Gelles, R.J. (1992). A profile of violence toward children. *Child Abuse and Neglect: The International Journal,* 17, 197–212.

Chapter 4

The Mad That We Feel

by Fred Rogers and Hedda Sharapan

A five-year-old boy once asked, "What do you do with the mad that you feel when you feel so mad you could bite?" I learned a lot about anger just from listening to his question.

One thing I heard in his question was a reminder that children can have intense angry feelings, too. Their anger, like ours, comes as a reaction to other feelings, for example, when they feel small, inadequate, or they feel left out, hurt, or disappointed. Those feelings are painful…they are legitimate…and they are very much a part of childhood.

There was more in that boy's question, though, than just telling me there were times when he felt really mad. His main concern seemed to be finding out how grown-ups find control at angry times.

That can be an especially important concern for four- and

five-year-olds. At that time in their lives, children are working hard to find control over all kinds of impulses. They're old enough to recognize what they're supposed to do and not do, but their inner controls are still weak. It can be hard for them to hold back their destructive urges when they're angry and upset.

After all, children aren't born with control. That's something they develop and learn—with a lot of support and encouragement from parents, child-care providers, and teachers.

One way we help is by offering just what that five-year-old was asking: alternatives to biting, hitting, and hurting. I told him that different people find different ways to handle their anger. For me, I said, it helps to play loud on the piano or even just to say, "I'm mad."

It can help children to hear about and see adults whom they know using constructive outlets when they're angry. How we, ourselves, express our anger will influence our children a great deal, as will our reactions to stories or what we see on television. But it can take a long while for children to develop adult "tools," like using words or finding a constructive outlet in music or art or something physical.

Words are such an important way for adults to express our feelings, but young children act on a much more primitive level. The outlets that seem to work best for most children (after they begin to develop some inner controls) involve physical activity. For example, some children let out their anger by doing a kind of temper-tantrum dance or by running fast. Others scribble harsh lines with crayons or markers or make pictures of angry faces and angry things. In many families, hammering nails or pounding clay or dough are acceptable forms of release.

Perhaps one of the most important things adults can do for children's early struggles with anger is to set limits: losing control is scary for children, and it helps them feel safe when we adults are firm about what we will and will NOT allow.

In setting those limits, though, we need to acknowledge children's rights to be angry; it's only what they do with that anger that we need to control. For example, if there's a new baby in the family, parents could clearly and firmly tell an older child, "I can understand that you're angry about the baby, but I can't let you hurt her." It could help to add: "I wouldn't want anyone to hurt you, either."

Acknowledging children's angry feelings can have some surprising results. A mother told us about a time she was forcibly holding the refrigerator door closed so that her four-year-old could not open it to get a snack. "It's too close to dinnertime," the mother insisted. The rage and determination on the little girl's face was so intense that her mother couldn't help bursting out laughing. "Jessica, I do believe you are angrier than I am," she said, and at that, Jessica's anger broke into laughter, too. It may have been a relief that her mother understood what she was feeling, or it may have been the unexpectedness of her mother's reactions, but in any event, the tension between them subsided.

Anger is a difficult feeling for most people—painful to feel and hard to express. But having angry feelings is a part of being human. We can't expect our children never to be angry, any more than we can ask that of ourselves, but we can help them find healthy outlets for the mad that they feel…and help them know the good feeling that comes with self-control.

"What Do You Do with the Mad That You Feel?"

What do you do with the mad that you feel
When you feel so mad you could bite?
When the whole wide world seems oh, so wrong
And nothing you do seems very right?
What do you do? Do you punch a bag?
Do you pound some clay or some dough?
Do you round up friends for a game of tag?
Or see how fast you can go?

It's great to be able to stop
When you've planned a thing that's wrong
And be able to do something else instead . . .

When I wrote that song, I took the first two lines right from the question that the five-year-old boy had asked.

Young children don't have many ways to express their feelings when they're upset. They don't use words well yet, and they don't have highly developed controls. Even though biting is a primitive way of saying, "I'm angry," it's sometimes one of the only ways a very young child has to begin with. The happy thing is that children can learn not to bite! They can learn to develop controls. (Of course, that learning happens best when it's through a loving relationship with an adult.)

The song expresses three basic ways we can help children deal with their angry feelings.

Understanding That Anger Is Natural and Normal

Everybody gets angry sometimes—even I do! When people ask if I ever get angry, I tell them, "Of course, I do!" And the most natural way for me to express my feelings is through the piano and through physical exercise.

Finding Healthy Outlet for Angry Feelings

Children don't have to bite or hit or hurt. There are other things they can do that don't hurt. Most importantly, as they grow, they can learn to use words to say, "I'm mad!" or "Stop that!" If parents and teachers can help a child say, "I'm angry because you took my toy," they're giving that child a powerful tool because words can help them start talking about ways to resolve the conflict—ways that don't hurt.

We can also help children channel their angry energies in other healthy ways, like making an angry picture, or building a block building to knock over, or banging an angry "song" on a xylophone, or pounding play clay into an angry "sculpture."

Helping Children Find Control and Not Hurt People or Ruin Things When They're Angry

Children need to know it's NOT all right to hurt someone or destroy something when they're upset. We often hear from people who work with young children that the ones who are most aggressive are the ones who are most scared. When we help children feel safe, they won't need to be so ready to protect themselves with fighting and "weapons."

It's a life-long challenge developing ways to deal "with the mad that we feel." Those who care for children early on by helping them develop loving, healthy inner controls are offering them one of the great gifts of their lives.

Activities to Work Out Angry Feelings

It can take a long while for children to develop controls and to be able to use healthy outlets when they're angry. Here are activities that can help along the way by giving children practice at stopping or staying on track or by giving them experiences with different constructive alternatives.

Try exercising!

Sometimes physical exercise can help children feel better when they are frustrated. If you put some active music on the radio or tape player, ask your child to follow your lead in doing some exercises, like:

- raising their hands over their heads
- lifting their knees for marching
- touching head, shoulders, toes
- making circular movements with their arms
- twisting from side to side
- jumping with one foot or two feet

It's important to follow fast-paced moving with some quiet music for calming down.

Try hand-tracing!

When young children hit, they often don't understand that their hands are hurting someone else. They are just learning about where their bodies begin and end. Hand-tracing can help children have a better sense of their own body boundaries—just in having the pencil or crayon move around the outside edges of their hands.

Trace your child's hands on a piece of paper. Then ask your child to help you make a list of many things people do with their hands—things that help them or other people.

Talk to you child about other ways he can use his hands such as:

- drawing pictures
- squeezing lemons
- pounding dough
- stirring food
- holding books or turning the pages in a book while reading

Try a Stop-n-Go musical game!

Play some music on the radio or tape. Ask your child to start dancing, and then to stop whenever you stop the music. Hurrah for your child! To be able to stop. That's not easy, and it can be practice for stopping biting or hitting later on at angry times.

Try stop signs!

When children use their hands to make their toy cars stop, they're practicing what it feels like to control their own feelings.

With markers, draw a road on an old sheet or on shelving paper. Ask your child to help you make stop signs for the roadway—by pasting the sign on a craft stick or pencil. The stick can stand upright if you anchor it in some play clay or modeling dough.

Try making play clay!
When children are angry, if you feel they have some controls, you could encourage them to do something with the mad that they feel, like pounding and making something from play clay. Here's an easy recipe for that:

1 cup water
2 cups flour
1 cup salt (Note: Because of the salt content, it is recommended that the salt be decreased if young children may put this mixture in their mouths)
1 teaspoon vegetable oil

Your child might want to help you mix these ingredients. If you'd like, you could add food coloring for some variation. If you store the play clay in an airtight container, you can keep it for any other times your child feels like he or she wants or needs it.

Try clap and stomp rhythms!
Make a sign that has CLAP on one side and STOMP on the other. When the sign says CLAP, lead preschoolers to clap. When the sign says STOMP, lead them to stomp. Guide preschoolers to make up rhythms by clapping and stomping. Begin by giving them a couple of rhythms, like:

-clap, clap, clap, stomp, stomp;
-clap, stomp, clap, stomp, clap;
-clap, clap, clap, stomp, stomp, stomp.

Then let every child take turns making a pattern that everyone else follows.

What Can Families Do?

Plan for warm and caring times together.

One of the best ways parents help children learn to handle angry feelings is by building a warm and trusting relationship with their children. When there's a close bond, children are more likely to try to please their parents. It's within a loving family that we all learn to control our behavior.

- Spend quiet time together, reading a book or sharing stories.
- Make up a simple song about how your child might be feeling.
- Ask your child about his or her day—maybe ask, "What was the best thing that happened to you today?"

Talk about angry feelings.

When children know their parents care deeply about them and care about whatever they're feeling, they are more likely to talk about feelings rather than act them out in hurting ways.

- When you've had a frustrating day, you could say, "I am really angry today because…"
- When your child seems to be angry, you could say, "I

know you're mad about that, but you can't hurt!" Don't you feel better when someone says, "I understand why you're mad" or "You have a right to be angry"?

- When your child is getting angry with a friend, you could say, "Tell him that you're angry. It helps when you use words."
- At a quiet time, talk about things children can do when they're angry so they won't hurt anyone or break things.

Help develop controls.
It takes time for children to learn to stop from doing something that will hurt others. It's scary for children to be out of control, and they need their parents to help them develop controls.

- Toddlers (or preschoolers who are very upset) often need to have adults firmly and caringly hold them or take them away from the situation.

- Think about saying "I'm proud of you" when your child is about to hit, but holds back and finds control.

- Help your child practice stopping and starting by playing games like "Red Light, Green Light" or "Stop and Go."

- Children also learn self-control when they do activities that need careful concentration, like stringing beads, moving toy cars along a "road" made from a piece of tape, or using snap-together toys.

Find healthy outlets.
When children have some controls, then they're more able to

channel their energies when they're angry. Parents can encourage healthy outlets by offering things like:

- crayons and paper for painting a mad picture
- play clay for kneading or pounding
- pounding toys
- musical instruments like drums or xylophones
- construction paper to tear for collages
- puppets for making up plays

Application and Reflection

1. What are three basic ways to help young children deal with their anger?

2. Think of some other activities that you could do with young children to help them deal with their angry feelings. Write your ideas below and try these with your child or group of preschoolers.

3. Who are the angry preschoolers that you know? How can you help them?

About the Writers

Fred Rogers is host and creator of *Mister Rogers' Neighborhood* on the Public Broadcasting System. Hedda Sharapan is associate executive producer of the program.

Chapter 5

Dealing with Illnesses, Disease, and Death

by Grace Ketterman

Recently a large corporation did a study to discover if families in which both parents worked outside the home were likely to have major problems. Overall, they felt that kids could adapt to such a situation without major damage.

The one area of concern, however, turned out to be that of illness in the children. Fathers were shocked to think that they should ever miss work to attend to a sick child. Their employers were not accustomed to men staying at home with a child. The mothers considered this concept to be grossly unfair. Why should they be the ones who always missed work to care for a sick child?

The truth is, no one really wants to stay at home with a fretting, ill child. Although some parents are able to stay at home to make special meals while they are sick and tend to other needs, many parents feel it is a burden to tend to a sick child. Others simply cannot afford to miss work and stay at home.

Fortunately with the Family Leave Act, working moms and dads can stay at home when a child is not well. And medical science offers excellent diagnostic skills and treatment regimes. If sick children's recoveries depended on just the care and nursing skills of parents, we'd be in deep trouble. But we are blessed with such resources so the burden of illness on parents is greatly reduced in most cases.

Here are the major physical systems of the human body and some of the most common diseases that afflict children and worry parents.

The Integumentary System
(skin, hair, and nails)
Diseases of the skin are caused by bacteria, viruses, fungus, insect and plant toxins, and injuries or accidents.

Bacterial infections: Examples of skin diseases caused by bacteria include impetigo, cellulitis caused by strep germs, and boils and sties caused by staph bacteria. These are red, painful, either spreading or localized rashes. They need to be diagnosed by your doctor and treated thoroughly.

Problems: Many germs are developing a resistance to the medications that may be life-saving. Be certain to give all the medicine your doctor prescribes.

Viral infections of the skin are commonly known as cold or fever sores. They are seen as red blisters about the mouth and nose. The blisters break easily and spread quickly. Youngsters who suck their fingers or bite their nails can spread this infection to their hands. Most of these sores heal fairly soon, but if not, ask your doctor to advise you. Some fairly effective anti-viral medicines are available.

Problems: Most children put everything in their mouths. Toys or objects can spread viral infections to others quickly. Keep such objects away from others and sterilize them carefully.

Fungus infections are known as athlete's foot or ringworm. There are a few others, not common in preschoolers. Such infections are very contagious but very treatable. Your doctor should prescribe what you use.

Problems: Fungi thrive and grow in warm moist areas like feet, skin, and bathrooms. If anyone in the family has such an infection, you must dry and disinfect your bathroom after each bath or shower until the entire family is well. While athlete's foot can be cured by "over the counter" medicines, ringworm often requires a careful diagnosis and prescription from your doctor.

Insect bites and plant irritants: Mosquitoes and chiggers are everywhere and cause red, itchy welts anywhere they alight. Due to the unavoidable scratching of children, they easily become infected. The use of anti-itching medicines can help shorten the time these last.

Stinging insects like wasps, bees, and hornets cause severe pain and swelling. If a child happens to have an allergic reaction, he or she may develop serious problems that can be life-threatening. Don't hesitate to call your doctor.

Spider bites are rare, but they can be very serious. Fortunately, most kids are afraid of spiders, so they avoid them. Spiders can disappear quickly so you may not realize a child is bitten. A serious spider bite causes an angry red welt that may have areas that are white. They are very painful. If you have any doubt, call your doctor.

Many plants can irritate the skin, but the most common ones are poison ivy, sumac, and poison oak. Find a book with pictures that clearly identify such plants and keep your children away from them. The itching they cause in the skin is horrible and lasts for at least 7 to 10 days. Your doctor can prescribe medication, but it is far easier to prevent than treat.

Accidents and injuries to the skin are extremely common in kids. Burns, scrapes, and cuts are a constant hazard. Do your best to keep hot things away from your children, also sharp items. If your child does suffer such an injury, seek medical advice. You may prevent ugly scars or serious infections by prompt attention.

Problems: Be certain your child's immunizations are up to date. Tetanus, a deadly infection, can result from wounds that occur out of doors.

Diseases of the Musculoskeletal System
(bones, joints, tendons, and muscles)

Bacterial infections in these parts of the body are not common. Osteomyelitis (an infection in a bone) used to strike terror into the hearts of both doctors and parents. Now, however, it is rare and can usually be readily cured with appropriate antibiotics. Be sure to have your doctor check any child who complains of pain and shows tenderness to pressure over a bone, especially in the wake of a fall, or an infection elsewhere in the body.

Viral infections can very easily afflict the muscles and joints. Any serious cold is likely to create aching in both muscles and joints. The only treatments useful for most such infections are rest, warmth, and pain relievers. Rarely, a doctor may prescribe one of the newer anti-viral medications.

Problem: Young children can't describe their pain or even tell you where they ache. If your child has a low grade fever and is "grouchy," try the correct dose of a pain reliever such as children's acetaminophen while waiting for your doctor's advice. Caution: The use of aspirin for a child under five years of age is not recommended.

Injuries: Any active child will fall, twist, or bump his or her body frequently. Rarely they may suffer a fracture of any involved bone. The pain, swelling, and distortion of such an injury will enable most parents to diagnose a broken bone.

But don't be fooled! A slight fracture may deceive you; any additional pressure or another simple fall can turn it into a truly serious injury. If your child complains of pain or winces when you touch a bruised spot, you should call your doctor. An X-ray is costly, but not nearly as expensive as a neglected fracture.

Sprains and bruises are common, rarely are serious, and usually treated with rest, support, and tender loving care.

Severe muscle cramps or aching can occur if a child is too active for too long a time. Gentle massages and cold or warm packs alternately will help heal such pains.

Tumors of the bone and cancer may occur in a child. If your child has chronic pain and some swelling over any bone area, do not wait. A simple X-ray can diagnose a problem. Early diagnosis and proper treatment can cure many forms of cancer.

The Endocrine System
(pituitary, thyroid, parathyroid, adrenal glands, ovaries or testes, and pancreas)

In young children, problems with this system are very rare; however, diabetes can occur in very young children. This is more likely if there is a strong family history of diabetes. If your child develops excessive thirst and urinates too much, be sure to have him or her checked for diabetes.

Early diagnosis and control can prevent the serious complications of a neglected case.

The thyroid gland can cause difficulty in even newborn babies. When it secretes too little of its hormone, thyroxin, a child's skin becomes very dry, the hair is coarse and falls out easily, the child has little energy, tires easily, and may have trouble thinking or responding normally. Once again, the diagnostic test is easy and treatment is effective.

The Digestive System
(stomach, intestines, and digestive organs)

Infections of any part of this system are common in children. Both bacteria and viruses can infect the mouth and throat. They easily spread to the stomach and intestines, causing vomiting and diarrhea. Care is crucial to be sure the child does not become dehydrated.

Over- and under-eating are worrisome to most parents. Preschoolers rarely have serious eating disorders like adolescents may have. They do, however, get into huge power struggles with parents who are too rigid in their expectations of eating habits. Follow your doctor's feeding regimen for your child; offer your child the healthy foods he needs. Make those foods as appealing as you can. Let him eat what he needs, and make him wait for the next scheduled eating time. Each child has a God-given regulator that tells him what foods, and how much, his body needs. Trust this and don't start the food fights that can become huge family battles. Of course, you will weigh your child once in a while. If you are concerned, have a talk with your doctor.

Other digestive system diseases are fairly rare—hepatitis (a liver infection) is fairly well known; constipation can be an annoyance; pinworms are fairly common and easily treated; stomach aches are often due to intestinal upsets from foods or "stomach" flu.

Eating or drinking toxic substances can cause severe vomiting or diarrhea. Be very careful to keep all medicines and any household chemicals well away from youngsters. If you suspect the child may have taken something harmful, do not wait. Get medical help at once! Keep the local poison control number near your telephone.

The Circulatory System
(heart and blood vessels)

The most common disease of this system in young children is some type of congenital malformation. These include defects in the walls that form the four chambers of the heart, abnormalities of the valves that open and close as blood is pumped through the various chambers; and strictures of various blood vessels leading to or from the heart. Fortunately, surgical procedures have been developed and perfected that make many such abnormalities completely curable. It seems impossible that such intricate surgery could be done on such tiny human beings. Sometimes we fail to realize that miracles come in various forms. The miracle of knowledge and technology that God has revealed to His children has transformed the quality of life for all of us.

Some infections afflict both the heart and the blood vessels. These are rare. Blood poisoning can result from the spread of an infection on the skin or elsewhere, causing an infection of the heart or blood vessels. Such an infection can be fatal, so all infections need to be treated promptly.

One of the most dreaded diagnoses in this system in the past was that of leukemia, cancer of the white blood cells. This is now treatable and some forms have greater than a 90 percent cure rate.

The Respiratory System
(nose, throat, lungs and their branches)

It has often been said that mankind can now explore space and distant planets, but has not found a cure for the common cold! And it's true. The bane of every parent's life is just that—a long-lasting, grouch-producing cold. Colds are caused by a variety of viruses that first affect the nose, sinuses, and throat of their unhappy victim.

In youngsters, the infection easily spreads to the ears, the trachea (windpipe), and the bronchial tubes. It may even penetrate the lung tissue itself, causing pneumonia. Earaches cause sleeplessness, severe pain, and temporary loss of hearing. They can be exhausting to parents as well as painful to a child. Fortunately, antibiotics and other medicines cure earaches quickly.

Croup is a frightening form of a cold. In this illness, the vocal cords become inflamed and swollen, causing difficulty in breathing. There is a constant, racking cough that sounds like the bark of a seal. It seems croup always attacks its victims at night, scaring both parents and patient. Immediately placing the croupy child in a bathroom with the shower on usually provides relief. The high humidity, especially with cool water or a cold-air humidifier, reduces the swelling and irritation and provides relief. Occasionally, a child with croup has to be placed in the hospital. This illness is one that will make you call your doctor. In most cases, recovery is rapid.

Asthma is another disease that affects the respiratory system. It is an allergic reaction that affects most of the body's systems, but its primary target is the tiny air sacs of the lungs (called alveoli). These are the places where fresh air is exchanged for carbon dioxide, a waste product of the body's metabolism. Tiny muscles contract, squeezing out "old" air, and expand, taking in fresh air. In asthma, these tiny muscle fibers tend to stay tightly contracted, so this normal exchange of air cannot take place. Breathing becomes labored and the patient feels exhausted.

We are not certain why, but there is an increase in this disease. It also seems to be more severe. So be sure to have your child carefully examined. Find out the cause of the allergy that causes it and be sure to have the proper medicines, prescribed by your doctor, on hand at all times.

Accidents and injuries can also occur in this system. The most common is choking caused by objects or food particles that can become lodged in the throat over the larynx. Such objects block the air flow through the vocal cords that normally close during swallowing to prevent choking. If a child happens to draw a deep breath as she or he starts to swallow, it can draw the object into the larynx or trachea instead of the esophagus.

Choking can terrify both child and parents. You must react quickly; turn the child upside down and squeeze the chest carefully but firmly. Pressure over the abdomen (the well-known Heimlich maneuver) can also work to dislodge the item and free it. If anyone is with you, they should call for emergency help if you are not able to relieve the child in a few seconds.

Choking is far easier to prevent than to remedy. Keep all small objects out of toddlers' reach and teach older children to put nothing in their mouths but food that can be carefully chewed.

Cystic fibrosis is a congenital disease affecting the lungs. It occurs in 1 out of 2,000 live white births and in only 1 in 17,000 black babies. It is rare in other ethnic groups. It is treatable, but not curable and is known to be passed on to the next generation. A great deal of research has revealed much about treatment and the improvement of the length and quality of life.

The Nervous System
(brain, spinal cord, and nerves)

Headaches are the number one ailment of this system. They usually accompany or signal the onset of infections. Colds, bronchitis, earaches, strep throats, flu, and all of the childhood diseases have headaches as one of their symptoms. But headaches may also be a sign of anxiety or tension in a child's life. Preschoolers rarely seem to complain of headaches, perhaps because they haven't the words to describe them. School-aged children, on the other hand, often complain of headaches and stomachaches that we find are clearly a sign of worry and too many pressures on their lives.

Infections of the brain and nervous system are, thankfully, rare. But most parents panic at the idea of meningitis or encephalitis. These are viral or bacterial infections of the tissues surrounding the brain or of the brain itself. There are excellent treatments for these illnesses, but death can be the outcome in severe cases.

Injuries of a severe sort are also relatively rare, but can cause total disabilities or serious crippling. Constant observation is a must for preschoolers as well as consistent discipline. Children as young as one year can be taught to stay within safe boundaries, but they always need adults close by to make sure they don't forget.

Birth injuries or genetic abnormalities are tragic events that cripple far too many children—rare as they are. Cerebral palsy, epilepsy, and a variety of neuro-muscular defects are still severely handicapping conditions that have little or no treatment available. Parents face the immense problem of conquering their grief and helping the child maximize the abilities he or she does have. At the end of this chapter you will find more about coping with disabilities.

The Genital and Renal System
(sexual organs, kidneys and urinary bladder)

Birth defects of these systems include malformation of the penis, undescended testes, rare abnormalities of the urinary bladder, and very rare abnormalities of the ovaries and uterus. Very rare is a Wilms' tumor that forms in the kidneys before birth. It is malignant but with early discovery and good treatment, the cure rate is excellent. It is usually diagnosed before the age of five but may grow so slowly it's not found until much later.

Infections of the kidneys and bladder are quite common in children. Girls have a shorter and more exposed access to the bladder, so careless toilet habits can allow germs to get into the bladder, causing cystitis. This causes severe pain during and after urination, the urine is cloudy and may look bloody. Should your child show such signs, contact your doctor at once. Prompt treatment of a bladder infection will prevent the spread of an infection to the kidneys where it becomes a very serious illness.

In today's sexually focused world, children often discover and explore their own and each other's genitalia. They may even insert objects into their own or a playmate's penis or vagina. I have had several reports of such events in preschools. Such activities are obviously emotionally loaded, but they also cause a high risk of infections or serious injuries.

If your child seems to be too focused on his or her own genitals, try to find out whether there is exposure to sexual molestation by another. Staying calm and seeking God's wisdom can prevent making such an event a crisis. Please don't become overly upset if you do discover such an event. Keep calm in front of the child. Do consult your doctor, and stop the contact with such an offender at once. If your doctor advises it, consult a good Christian children's counselor and follow his or her advice. The law does require that you report any such event to your state's department of child welfare.

The old fear of infections in boys' testes is nearly eliminated by proper immunizations. We used to worry a lot about the childhood disease of mumps, which often spread to the testes. This could cause sexual sterility in severe cases. But we rarely see a case of mumps these days. Along with measles, rubella, tetanus, and chicken pox, mumps has been nearly wiped out in our country.

A severe blow to the mid-back area can cause bruising of a kidney. This could occur from a fall or from being hit very hard. Teach your children not to hit or hurt each other. If a serious blow happens, your child will feel severe pain and there will be some blood in the urine. If you suspect such an injury, consult your doctor at once.

The Lymphatic System
(lymph nodes and vessels)

This system serves two purposes. One is the protection of the body's tissues from certain infections. The other is to help provide fluid and nutrients to the tissues of the body.

If you have felt your own or your child's neck during a severe cold or strep throat, you no doubt discovered firm lumps under the jaw, chin, and the back of the neck. These lumps are lymph nodes or glands that have become enlarged during the body's process of fighting off an infection nearby. They are really little heroes that suffer inflammation themselves in protecting the rest of the body.

Now sometimes they are the location of serious infections themselves.

Infectious mononucleosis, known simply as "Mono," is a well-known example of this. Lymph glands all over the body (but mainly on the head and neck) become enlarged, feel firm, and are tender. Since this seems to be caused by a virus, most doctors treat it only with rest. Healing is usually complete within one to four weeks. Rarely, severe cases may occur with various complications.

Cancer of the lymphatic system is, fortunately, very rare in children. New treatments for cancer are encouraging.

Injuries to this system occur mainly through extensive infections or injuries that can leave scarring of the lymphatic channels. If this is severe, a patient may develop what we call lymphedema. The fluids that should flow through these channels are blocked and collect in the tissues around the injured area. Such swelling (edema) is rarely dangerous, but it is unattractive and uncomfortable.

The Sensory System
(sight, hearing, taste, touch, motion, and position)

The sensory system will function naturally but it's up to parents to tie it to the emotional and mental functioning of a child. You must share your own ecstasy at the sight of an evening star, a rainbow, the rumble of thunder, the smell of a flower, the touch of a butterfly or even an inchworm crawling across a hand. Your drawing attention to sensory stimulation will teach your child to take delight in his or her senses. Through our senses we connect with all nature, God the Creator, and His other children.

Allergies, colds, and other infections may temporarily damage some of our senses. It is amazing to remember, however, that God made our bodies so they tend toward health. Time, patience, and excellent medical care will nearly always provide recovery.

Considering the intricacies of the human body, it is surprising that anyone can be perfect. There are many defects that are present at birth. In the sensory system these are so tragic. It is grievous to see a child born blind or deaf, or missing any other sense or function. It is well known, however, that when a sense or function is missing or lost, some other part of the body helps compensate. A blind child, for example, usually develops extra-sensitive hearing and smell. Children with physical disabilities often show superbly sensitive, loving spirits. So we must learn to accept what we are given, grieve what is lacking, and make the most possible of what we have—in ourselves and in our children.

No matter how trivial an illness may seem, definite signs when you should call your doctor are:

- A prolonged fever that does not disappear in a day or two.
- A high fever, 101 degrees F or higher.
- An earache, along with a cold.
- Labored breathing and a persistent cough, even without fever.
- Severe stomach pain, especially if localized in the right, lower area of the abdomen and with fever.
- Any sign of a urinary tract infection.
- Any skin infection that gets hot, red and you see red streaks radiating into surrounding tissues.
- Any injury that suggests a broken bone, internal injury, or indication of the need for stitches.
- Any time you are worried about a specific sign or symptom your child evidences.

Consult your doctor or a family medical encyclopedia for more information on these illnesses.

Coping with Death

Sooner or later everyone has to learn the real facts of life— and death is one of those facts. Too many parents try to protect their children from the mystery and pain of death. Some parents have awakened pet store owners at night in an effort to replace a dead gerbil or kitten!

It is extremely difficult, then, to help a youngster deal with the loss of a dearly loved grandparent, a parent, perhaps a sibling, or even his or her own death. Yet this is one of the opportunities of a Christian parent. Considering some of the least difficult losses first, here are some ideas to help teach your child lifelong lessons:

Loss of a Pet

If your family's dog, cat, or other pet dies, help your child become a part of the process. Ask your veterinarian to explain the illness or injuries that took that pet's life. If possible, have your children help bury the animal and/or conduct a simple memorial service. Try to discuss the tender, worrisome, or funny memories related to that pet. Allow the children to cry, and grieve with them. Listen to their anger and blame, but help them get beyond these and teach them not to get stuck in feelings of guilt—even if their carelessness may have been a factor in the death (e.g. letting a pet out of a fenced area). Teach children that God cares about how they feel when they lose a pet.

Death in the Family

Usually, family deaths are the result of some illness, more or less prolonged. In such situations, parents have some opportunities to prepare children. They should be told, in simple terms, that Uncle John or Grandma is very sick and may die. Usually, children are comforted to see that ill person. If, however, they are badly disfigured, connected to the array of tubes hospitals use, or are too emaciated to be recognized, you may be wise to avoid contact. Showing a recent photograph of that loved one can be wiser than a visit. If the sick person is able to enjoy them, help your child color a picture or write a love note and take or send them to that relative.

Avoid saying things like God took this dear one. That can convey to a child that God is mean. Instead, explain that this life is God's gift to us to help us get ready for heaven. There is a right time for each one to die, and God knows that time. Assure the child that God cares about his sadness and will comfort him.

Any child old enough to talk will gladly talk about what Uncle Jim was like. He laughed, played, liked pumpkin pie, and was a good swimmer. In other words, a child can vividly describe who Uncle Jim was and what he was like. These personality traits, loves, and dislikes describe Uncle Jim.

Depending on a child's maturity, parents can decide when a child is old enough to attend a funeral. Be honest, and help the child understand what is happening at the funeral.

When a Child Dies

Unfortunately, children do die. Their illnesses can be quite prolonged, and often they have a sense about imminent death.

A father of such a dying child was confronted by his son's question, "Daddy, what's it like to die?" The heartbroken father desperately sought God's guidance. What could he possibly know about dying? God gave him this comforting answer. "Son," he said, "when you were just a little boy, you used to fall asleep in front of the TV, watching your favorite tape. I would pick you up in my big, strong arms and carry you to your bed and tuck you in. Next morning, you woke up in a different room. I think that's how dying is. Jesus will just pick you up in His really strong arms, and take you to heaven with Him. He'll take care of you until Mama and I get to heaven to be with you again!"

What a wise and comforting example of the truth. Jesus has promised to never leave us nor forsake us. He will see each one through the valley of the shadow of death. And He will give those who are bereaved His special comfort and healing. As you teach your child about death, you will become stronger in your faith.

Caring for a Sick Child

In today's world, a prolonged illness is rare in children. But even a day or two can seem long when a child has a high fever, cough, sore throat, or stomachache. Here are some ideas to keep on file if your child needs bed rest and extra care:

- Be sure you have good communication with your doctor and nurse. Write out their orders and organize the giving of medications. Be sure to keep a record of temperatures, fluid and food problems, and whatever they request to follow your child's progress.
- Balance tender, loving care with tough, loving care. Most kids will feel better at times and whine to get up and play. Until your doctor OKs this, you must be firm. Take charge in a no-nonsense manner.
- Keep a "Rainy Day Box" with toys, books, and materials

for crafts. Rotate a few old toys into such a box; they will seem like old friends rediscovered. Sort out items a sick child could enjoy while propped up in bed. Make a sickbed table out of an old cardboard box by cutting out semicircles on two sides. It will fit over the child's hips and legs and allow coloring, painting, or propping up books.

- Without pampering, fix a few special treats for your child. Even kids with stomach flu can enjoy gelatin, carbonated beverages, and toast or crackers. Cut out the center of a slice of bread with a cookie cutter and place a little wedge of cheese on the cracker.

- Do not worry about food for a day or two. God made us in a wondrous way—when our bodies are ready for food, our appetites will return and kids, especially, soon take in enough calories to make up for those lost in the illness.

- Liquids are another matter. The body loses a great deal of fluid when there is a fever, diarrhea, and vomiting. And these are all likely in children's illnesses. Try a variety of fluids as allowed by your doctor. Wait an hour or so after vomiting has stopped, and offer only a few sips at a time. Sodas, juices, weak tea, or liquid gelatin may be tried. As soon as your child will tolerate it, offer an ounce of liquids every hour, gradually increasing the amount and shortening the time between sips.

- Have hope! Even missing a night's sleep will not seriously harm you. Do not let your fatigue make you irritable with your patient. You will recover when she gets well. And you'll be so glad you used this time of sickness to demonstrate your love, protection, and strength to a helpless child. Remaining patient and loving is an excellent way to model God's unconditional love.

- If the child is small enough, and your doctor OKs it, hold and rock him as much as possible. Your nearness and gentle motion are soothing and healing and will strengthen your bonding.
- When you are weary of a convalescing child, try to remember she will soon be well. This phase is often the worst. The child is tired, bored, feels more energetic, but is still not really well. Allow a child in this stage of recovery a bit more activity and assure her that gradually she will be well again.

Your child's illness can draw you closer or it can separate you by resentment. Chose your course wisely.

Preparing for a Hospital Stay

Most hospitalizations for children are very brief these days. A tonsillectomy used to require two or three days and a hernia repair even longer. Now less than a day is allowed. This is a mixed blessing. On one hand, the sooner a child is at home in his own bed, the sooner he feels secure and well. On the other hand, the possibility of an occasional complication can create real anxiety in parents. Be sure your doctor knows of your fears and get a promise that he will be available until you are confident that all is well.

Explain to your child as much as you can about your doctor's office and the hospital experience. The doctor or nurse will sometimes explain procedures to your child. Some fine short books about generalities in hospital stays are available. Check your library or bookstore for books that are age appropriate for your child.

Children always fear painful experiences. And parents instinctively try to protect them from pain. Nevertheless, everyone does better with honesty. Say: You are going to have the shot. It will hurt. You may cry if you like, but you must have this medicine to make (or keep) you well. I'll be here with you, so you know I'll comfort you. Soon the pain will go away. I'll help you be brave.

Your own confidence or anxiety will be clearly seen by your child, so don't try to fool him. Tell him you are anxious only because you care about him, but you will be brave, too. You'll be surprised how your honesty will even help you to be strong.

Today's Medical World

Technology development has revolutionized our world. The medical world has benefited hugely from modern discoveries. Consider the following.

Immunizations have wiped out smallpox, diphtheria, and nearly eliminated whooping cough, tetanus, measles, mumps, and rubella. Polio used to terrify youngsters as they saw friends crippled by or dead from polio. Rheumatic fever and heart disease, as well as nephritis (caused from complications of strep infections that cause inflamed kidneys) are all but gone since antibiotics were discovered. Surgery can now cure many birth defects. Organ transplants offer miracle cures where once death was slow but inevitable. Mechanical devices monitor bodily functions with extreme accuracy. This frees up nursing time that can be devoted to patient care and comfort.

When choosing health care, remember to:

- Be as selective as possible in choosing a health insurance company. If you are insured by your employer, exert any influence you can to require their selection of a plan with a heart.

- Speak with your doctor about your concerns in a thoughtful, non-defensive manner.

- Whenever you consult your doctor for an illness or medical concern, have your questions listed and state them clearly. Do not let her intimidate you. Be firm and persistent. You deserve the answers that will help you get well.

- Keep both your employer and your health insurance representative clearly informed of any and all problems you encounter in your quest for good medical care.

- Keep a balanced perspective regarding medical care, especially in life and death issues. It could be wrong to heroically try to sustain life when God knows it's time for that person to die. It seems even more wrong to give up on life-saving treatment when there is still hope for recovery or some quality of life.

Coping with Disabilities

You are already aware of the fact that due to birth defects, injuries, or severe illnesses some children are burdened with various disabilities. Any such problem affects the entire family, often in major ways. Often divorce is significantly higher between couples who have a child who is both blind and deaf. Apparently, one parent, usually the mother, devotes so much of herself to the child that her husband feels neglected, even unwanted at times. The opposite needs to be true. If you are a couple to whom God has entrusted a child with a disability, *draw close to one another* and to Him. Seek God's healing, wisdom, and guidance; if not healing of the disability, then healing of your grief over it. His Word is full of promises that He will supply all of your needs.

If you have been given a child with the challenge of a disability, the first response you are likely to experience is that of grief—in all of its dimensions. The stages of grief have been well studied. They are denial, blame and bargaining, anger, guilt, depression, resignation, and finally healing.

In the stage of denial you will try to believe the diagnosis is wrong. You will want to see many doctors and try all of the remedies you may hear about. Your faith can be sorely tried if you believe God will heal your child's malady, but He says no.

Do seek two or three evaluations, but if they all agree and your child does not improve, you may have to accept a tough fact of life. God does not promise to make life easy, but He does promise to share your burden. He always loves you.

A Jewish rabbi once said of us Christians that we make of God an order-taker. If He does not fill our orders as requested, we feel sad or angry and may even doubt Him. He told me that the Jewish family of faith simply asks God to see them through the vicissitudes He allows them to have. The rabbi may have a point. Sooner or later, we must bow to the truth, accept the facts, and move on.

The *anger/blame/bargaining* phase is understandable. "God," we pray, "if you will grant my child perfect sight (or even a little), I will serve You better!" We can blame God for the disability and stay angry with Him, severing the ties to our best resource! Sometimes we blame God for the mistakes of people or even the meanness of Satan. Be sure to know, in and from God there is no evil. He will redeem us and empower us, and always loves us.

How easy it is for us to blame ourselves for such problems! We can allow guilt to rob us of peace and destroy our joy. Rarely is a disability the fault of anyone. Genetic defects *do* exist. Accidents do happen. Birth injuries can't always be prevented. Even if you were careless or abused alcohol or drugs that caused a disability, you can be forgiven. That's why we all need the Savior. Seek His free forgiveness, accept His transforming grace, and then forgive yourself. Walk on with Him who will redeem you!

Blaming others for a disability is also tempting. We feel less helpless if we can make someone else responsible. Suing a doctor can make you feel powerful. But usually, doctors are not at fault. Use care and cool judgment before giving in to the temptation to blame anyone.

The *depressed stage* of grief is really the sad process of mourning. Wishing for what could or should have been, but isn't, makes any normal human being sad. In creeping through this stage of grief, find a time and a place to cry as much as you need to, and then cry with a friend. Cry out your anguish to your heavenly Father. When all of your feelings are expressed, resign yourself to the truth—however tragic that may be. Along with that resignation there returns a bit of peace and hope for ultimate healing. It is only then that one is ready for redemptive thinking and planning.

A number of examples on television recently verify the validity of this process. Individuals who were born with severe disabilities have found some area of usefulness in life. Those whose disabilities came from accidents discovered new spiritual resources and areas of service. In most cases these "victims" become conquerors through the support of parents and others who refused to become stuck in the helplessness of prolonged grief.

Granted, there are some disabled individuals for whom there is no hope for any area of service or usefulness. Hopefully, their very helplessness can create compassion in caretakers, community support and help for the family, and a profound gratitude for the existence of health in so many.

Many families with a child who has serious disabilities seem afraid to ask for help. One group of such parents feared that no one else would really be capable of handling the complex care that was needed. They did, however, devise a plan for helping each other. But you may be amazed at the many loving people who would be happy to care for your child, giving you time for each other and your children. This is a great area of service for any church to sponsor.

In conclusion, here are five basic principles to consider when facing illness, disease, and death:

- Illness and disease exist. Sooner or later, they strike every home and each individual. The challenge is to work toward recovery with the God-given tendency of the body to return to health and seek the help of medicine that God has also provided.

- Death, too, is a fact of life. We all dread to think of this reality. Grief is a painful process. But faith and biblical knowledge can enable us to transcend this ultimate sorrow and return to life. If the death is your own, be assured you will know eternal truth of life with the heavenly Father.

- In caring for sick children, parents must find the balances of tough and tender love, honesty about the pain to be endured, and the healing to be expected.
- Even in a "culture of death," mechanical and cold as it is, find a way to work with your doctor and your medical health insurance agency. Assume more than your share of responsibility. You will often have to be assertive, even demanding. So do it for the sake of your children and your whole family.
- When your child is less than perfect and suffers unfair limitations, work through your grief. Help your child struggle through his grief. Then move on to help the child make the most from the abilities he has.

Remember the Bible verse, "Suffer little children, and forbid them not, to come unto me: for of such is the kingdom of heaven" (Matthew 19:14, KJV). Picture Jesus surrounded by children. He didn't just hold them on His lap. More than likely He teased and chased those children with great energy. He would have gently touched those who were afraid and shy. And certainly He would have enabled them all to know they were safe in His absolute love.

Application and Reflection

1. What are the ten systems of the human body?

2. What are the most common and well-known diseases that afflict each system?

3. How can you decide when to call your doctor regarding a child's illness?

4. You are stuck with a health insurance company that seems unwilling to provide payment for a certain type of medical care you need. What can you do about this?

5. What are the stages of grief over any loss—death, illness, or disabilities?

6. How can you help friends, relatives, or a church family during a prolonged illness? How you help a family with a disabled child? What can your church do?

7. Write a letter to God telling Him how you feel about an illness, disease, or perhaps the death of a friend or family member.

8. Pray, seeking God's guidance and asking Him to help you cope with illnesses or deaths you may experience. Write your prayer in the space below or in a personal prayer journal.

About the Writer

Grace Ketterman is a physician and child psychiatrist and has served as the Medical Director of the Crittenton Center for children and adolescents in Kansas City, Missouri. She is also the author of several books dealing with child care and family issues from a Christian perspective.

Chapter 6

Family Issues

by Susan Allen

Many tough issues face today's families and because families are so different, a definitive solution to every problem is not available. However, understanding how these problems affect each member of the family can help lead to a solution. Let's take a close look at some of these tough issues and discover how to tackle them.

Divorce

"Every year, 1.2 million children see their parents divorce. Beyond the numbers, we should meet these children's needs because it's biblically sound. The Bible says in James 1:27 (NASB[1]) that 'this is pure and undefiled religion in the sight of our God and Father, to visit orphans and widows in their distress.'"[2] These modern-day orphans live among us, and we are called to love and minister to them.

Parents struggling with the issues of divorce want to do everything possible to shield their children from the pain they are experiencing. Though the intentions are admirable, avoiding the issue tends to add to the stress the child is likely already experiencing. Communication is critical to the child being able to know that you can be trusted to be honest, no matter how difficult the situation is.

Though the children are likely aware of the tension in the home, waiting to involve them until a final decision is made is best. Once the decision is made, however, have an honest and open discussion with them. When it is possible for both parents to be a part of the discussion, it is best for the children. When both parents are a part of the discussion, the children are assured that it is a joint decision rather than placing blame on one parent. A joint discussion also communicates that the parents will continue to work together to make decisions that affect the children. However, in a case of abandonment, or when the other parent refuses to be part of the discussion, it is far better for one parent to initiate the discussion than for the children to be left wondering what is wrong.

Children should be given a reason for the divorce. Left to their own conclusions, children will often think they are to blame. State clearly that they are not at fault in any way. Though you can explain to children that it is normal for them to want their parents to get back together, do not allow them to harbor false hopes that you will be reunited.

Children should be told what changes they can expect. Though you may not know all the answers, share information you have related to where they will live, how often they will see and talk with the noncustodial parent, and any other major life changes they will experience. Always assure children that they will be loved and cared for by both parents in the days ahead.

What are common fears that should be addressed in young children?

Changes in Family and Normal Way of Life

Change is always difficult and frightening. The divorce may mean a new home, new neighborhood, and new friends. Involvement with extended family members may change. A divorce usually means a move into a smaller home and less availability of financial resources. Maintain as much consistency as possible. The fewer changes the first year the better. Maintain as many rules and rituals as possible to minimize the degree of trauma for children. Because routines and familiarity bring comfort to preschoolers, care should be taken that children carry special comfort items between households.

Loss of Familiarity and Security

Children become attached to family members, pets, their home, their room, their church, their preschool. Stress can result from change in the amount of contact with any of these. In addition to visits, regular contact through letters, email, telephone calls, and exchange of pictures can ease the transition. Each parent should make every effort to encourage a healthy, loving relationship between the child and the other parent.

Children often grieve over the loss of relationships as they have known them. Parents should make every effort to maintain the children's contacts with extended family. If a change is necessary, look for steady, safe, dependable child care that can be constant in the child's life.

Children often feel angry, sad, lonely, insecure, abandoned, and afraid. It is important to share your faith and have your children see you live your faith as you lead your children to look to God for strength during this difficult time. Surround children with strong Christian adults who can give support as you seek to rebuild your lives.

Fear of Abandonment

The reality of the loss the preschooler is feeling causes fears of losing even more. David Elkind in *The Hurried Child* tells us "Divorce hurries children because it forces them to deal with separations that, in the usual course of events, they would not have to deal with until adolescence or young adulthood."[3] Because they have experienced this early loss, preschoolers often fear the loss of parents and worry about who will take care of them. Children of divorce often suffer from the loss of not one but two parents as the custodial parent often finds himself so emotionally drained from the divorce and the stress of single parenting that there is little or no energy left for parenting. These children are often forced to grow up quickly as they take on more and more adult responsibilities and often learn to relate to the parent as a partner.

Recognize that regression in previous accomplished tasks such as toilet training is normal during times of extreme stress.

Exercise patience in dealing with preschoolers as they struggle to move ahead. A preschooler may exhibit unusual amounts of stress if the parent is late picking her up from Sunday school or day care. Let adults who are involved with the child, such as baby-sitters, teachers at church, and other adults who are important in the life of your child know of the life changes as soon as possible so that they can be sensitive to the special needs of the child. Continually reassure the preschooler of your love and care. If a preschooler continues to show signs of distress, consult your doctor or pediatrician for a professional evaluation.

Hostility Between Parents

Most likely the child has experienced tension in the household long before the finality of the divorce. It is important that the preschooler not be drawn into the arguments and forced to take sides. Though we often hear that divorce is not as damaging as the life of conflict, this is not supported by the evidence. "For kids," according to University of Michigan psychologist and divorce expert Neil Kilter, "the misery in an unhappy marriage is usually less significant than the changes after a divorce. They'd rather their parents keep fighting and not get divorced."[4]

Children of divorce often experience the tensions of divided loyalty. Many children report that each parent tells them negative things about the other parent and encourages them to support them in the battle. Not only do the children lose in this scenario, but ironically the parents lose as well, as the children learn to play one parent against the other in efforts to obtain what they desire.

Regardless of your personal experiences, recognize the importance of the other parent in the life of your child. Speak positively of the other parent in front of your child. If differences arise, discuss these in the absence of your child. Avoid communicating to the other parent through your child. If you as parents cannot find a way to communicate appropriately to one another, seek a liaison to carry out communication regarding the welfare of the children. "Children will do best if they know that their mother and father will still be their parents and remain involved with them even though the marriage is ending and the parents won't live together. Research shows that children do best when parents can cooperate on behalf of the child."[5]

The reactions of preschoolers will vary with the personalities of each child. Some will express fear. Others may feel responsible and feel that he or she should be punished. Others may exhibit anger and aggressive behavior. Some may become sad and withdrawn. Nightmares may become more common.

Due to the prevalence of divorce in our society, even preschoolers from strong families fear divorce. As they watch the parents of their friends and relatives divorce and interact with so many children who live in single parent homes, they must wonder, "Will this happen to me?"

What Can Loving Adults Offer a Hurting Child?
Books
Stories can serve as a nonthreatening buffer to stress. Children often can deal with feelings by relating to the characters in a

story. Many wonderful books are available. *Why Don't We Live Together Anymore* by Robin Prince Monroe (HCP) is an excellent resource. Church media libraries should make available age-appropriate books for children to read. Parents can look for opportunities to hold the child close and read a book together. Allow time for conversation about the stories read. Sometimes children will shift from talking about the characters of the story to the comparison to their life. Parents can ask open-ended questions, such as: What did Ashley feel? Why did she feel that way?

Conversation

Parents should be available to converse with children often. Children should be assured that both parents love them deeply and always will. Acknowledge the feelings that children express. Be available to listen and respond in a way that avoids telling your child how to feel. Talk with your child on a "feeling" level. Rather than asking, "How was preschool today?" ask, "How do you feel about…?"

Children often fear they are the cause of the divorce and should always be assured that the problems are between the parents and that they are in no way responsible for the divorce. Be available to listen at times of transition between homes but do not force the child to share what he has experienced with the other parent. Put aside your own feelings to celebrate any special joys your child has experienced. Feelings can be shared as parents and children relive memories through family pictures or videos, giving value to the family history that is vital to the security of the child in this time of insecurity and loss.

Play

Young children often express their feelings best through play. Preschoolers should be given opportunities to express their feelings through dramatic play, play dough, sand or water play, and puppets. Some preschoolers will interact with a favorite doll or stuffed animal. Allow the child to play out her feelings. You may learn valuable information as you observe from a distance but do not interfere unless the child invites you to participate.

Make time to release tensions by playing together. When was the last time you enjoyed flying a kite on a windy afternoon? It only takes a few minutes to break out the bottles of bubbles and fill the house with fun and laughter. Who knows, when you break out the sidewalk chalk and begin decorating the driveway together the entire neighborhood may join in the fun! Crafting together seasonal items such as gingerbread houses, homemade valentines, or dying Easter eggs create wonderful memories.

What Can the Church Do?

"The reason God hates divorce is because he loves the family. The family is a place where we can understand the blessing of God. We need to love the family and hate divorce as much as God does. We also need to care for people broken by the pain of divorce, separation, and out-of-wedlock birth."[6]

The church needs to see itself as a hospital for sick marriages. Much less time is required in offering guidance in healing a sick marriage than in dealing with the disruption caused by a broken marriage. Churches should focus on offering models of healthy marriages as an example of the family as God intended, which many have never seen. Parents need the opportunity to gather with other Christians in discussion groups and seminars designed to strengthen healthy marriages and to teach parenting skills. The church should provide resources for both parents and children by providing appropriate books and videos in the church media library and by providing workshops, support groups, and study groups.

Sixty percent of children growing up in the United States today will spend part of their childhood living in a single-parent family. How will the church address the needs of these hurting kids? Neil Wiseman in *It Takes a Church* reminds us that, "Like nothing else, the church can be the family we don't have and a community that loves us even when we are not as lovable as we ought to be."[7] The church can be a place of substitute families when families are broken or nonexistent.

Children need loving teachers at church who care about the spiritual, physical, and emotional needs of each child. Church should be a haven from the tension and stress the child may be experiencing at home. Teachers and friends of children should speak kindly about both parents. Be sensitive in dealing with activities and themes concerning the home and the family and on special days such as Mother's Day and Father's Day. Look for opportunities to build the self-esteem of the child by showering the child with unconditional love and by focusing the child's attention on the things he can do well. Teachers should react lovingly and sensitively to children who may exhibit signs of stress through anger, withdrawal, or aggression. Activity areas such as homeliving where the child can act out his feelings, or resources such as play dough allow a preschooler opportunities to release frustration in acceptable ways.

Welcome single adults into your worship services. Simple acts such as learning and calling them by name will affirm their place in the body. Often single adults feel awkward and out of place in a congregation full of couples and families. Your warm greeting and an invitation to sit with your family can bring a sense of warmth and belonging to the spirit of a single parent. Recognize that single parents are often lonely and weary. Encourage families and couples to invite single parents and their children into their homes. Single parents with small children are often starved for adult companionship and conversation. Make yourself available to provide child care so that single parents can have a night out or organize a Parents Night Out for all parents in your congregation. A weary single parent could benefit from a gift certificate or scholarship that allows some time away from parenting responsibilities.

Many single parents may be in need of financial assistance to meet the basic needs of their family. Ministries to single mothers could include advice on financial matters or assistance with income tax forms. Some churches sponsor an auto day when single moms can receive assistance with basic maintenance, such as a tune-up or oil change. Others offer an organized ministry of members who can assist with basic home maintenance chores.

Application and Reflection

1. Think of your own church. Do the programs and activities meet the needs of single parents and their children?

2. Visit your church media library. Does it provide resources that will encourage and equip single parents and their children to grow in their walk with God and to find their place in the Body of Christ?

3. Pray, asking God to reveal to you a hurting child whom you can hold and bless and encourage as you affirm his gifts and promise to our world today.

Blended Families

As you think of the enormous needs of the families in your congregation, reflect on this quote: "If God is our Father, then the family to which we belong is bigger than a two-parent family or a single-parent family, or a blended family. The family, God's family, is bigger than you think."[8]

Kevin Leman, Ph.D., in his book *Living in a Stepfamily Without Getting Stepped On* writes, "Despite the odds against them, despite the bruising and shattering divorce (sometimes more than one) people remain intrepid eternal optimists who try marriage again. In America alone, over thirteen hundred new blended families form every day. And most of the men and women who take the plunge naively expect that this time their marriage and family life will work because they won't make the same mistakes. This time have found Mr. Right or Mrs. Wonderful, and they will live harmoniously blended ever after."[9]

One of the greatest problems faced by the blended family is the necessity of making all of the decisions at once. Everything from family chores to holiday traditions to curfew times are determined all at once. All of this takes place as not only families, but cultures, traditions, well established patterns of behavior, past histories, and even memories are also being blended.

Parents should recognize that stepchildren will likely challenge the authority of the stepparent from the beginning. A stepparent who walks in the door and immediately demands authority is likely to face many obstacles. Important tasks of shared parental authority are to define and maintain boundaries while together establishing roles and relationships for the new family unit. Allow time for family members to learn to trust one another. Through patience and communication, a trust for the individual style of parenting develops between the parents. Practice thoughtful and common courtesy among family members. Respect each individual's need for privacy and the need for children to cherish and display mementos of their relationship with the other parent and family.

The greatest need for blended families to succeed is for parents to make their marriage a priority. In an effort to keep the children happy and to win the approval of the children, many parents give their own relationship a backseat to their relationships with the children. As in first marriages, the most important relationship is the marriage relationship. Sit with the children early and make it clear to all that though nothing could change your love for the children, you now have the responsibility of also nurturing the marriage relationship. This relationship must take priority. Take care to calendar couple time in the busy times of your lives. You must nourish this young, tender relationship, and value it enough to schedule time for it to grow.

As in every family situation, attention to worship is critical. Early in the blending of the family, search together for a place of worship that will meet the needs of all. A church family can provide loving, nurturing adults who can provide relationships for both the parents and for the children.

Establish times of family worship. This time could be as simple as a brief time of prayer and Scripture around the breakfast table. Be careful not to use this time as an opportunity for you to "make a point" concerning family problems or to "preach" at your children. Let it be a simple time of joining together to pray for one another and for others outside of the family circle. What a special joy for parents to ask God's blessings upon their children as they go out to live their day. Even a short time of prayer just before the family leaves the house sets the tone for the day and brings blessings upon the family. As families come together in worship, they are joined into a common bond, and relationships are strengthened and nourished as the needs of each family member are brought to the Father.

Most important is the responsibility parents have been given to guide the family to focus on the things of God in every part of their life. In Deuteronomy 6:5–7 we are given the commandment, "And you shall love the Lord your God with all your heart, and with all your soul, and with all your might. And these words, when I am commanding you today, shall be on your heart; and you shall teach them diligently to your sons and shall talk of them when you sit in your house and when you walk by the way and when you lie down and when you rise up." These words apply to the blended families as well as the traditional. It is God's plan for parents to be faithful to pass their faith on to their children.

Bear in mind that the age of the children coming into the blended families is a critical issue. The blending of families with preschool children is typically easier, as they bring less family history and tradition into the blending of the new family. However, the blending of families with older children or teenagers has greater challenge, as they bring more developed personalities, relationship bonds, and family history into the making of the new unit. Some experts believe that it takes as much as two years before children begin to truly accept a stepparent. Clearly, these days of adjustment will require much patience and prayer on the part of the parents who so desperately want to be accepted.

Blended families can begin to create new family traditions by bringing the traditions they valued most before the blending and deciding which ones fit the one family best. Many children will continue to spend holidays and maintain traditions with noncustodial parents and/or grandparents. Blended families may want to plan carefully to establish their own holiday traditions when they can be together.

Another important step in creating a new family history is being careful to record special times through pictures and videos. Photos of family vacations, the family together as they celebrate the special achievements of a child, or photos of holiday celebrations all come together to form a larger picture of a family bonding together. As families create a record of these memories, they are recording a history of their time together. Times spent together looking at pictures and videos of happy times together create special bonds of family.

Recognize that it takes time to build relationships. Your preconceived ideas, stereotypes, or dreams of the perfect family or the "Brady Bunch" family can lead to disappointment. Forming family relationships will take great patience and time. Stepparents should look for opportunities to build relationships with the stepchildren. Being available to listen; being the encourager for the child in times of challenge; attending dance recitals, soccer games, and band concerts; and spending time shopping for the special dress for the prom are all important messages that you care about the child.

Many stepchildren benefit greatly from relationships formed within the new blended family. An only child longing for companionship may find a new place in a family of siblings that can bring joy and new opportunities for growth. Many children develop very close relationships with a stepparent, possibly filling a void where there is little or no relationship with the noncustodial parent. In the creation of the new blended family, the child develops a multitude of new relationships, offering opportunities for children to enjoy nurturing relationships with many more people, new step-cousins, aunts, uncles, and/or grandparents.

In creating your new family, continue to encourage your children in their relationships with the noncustodial parent. Encourage and assist where needed as they make or buy gifts for the noncustodial parent and other family members. Do everything you can to make transitions from one household to the other as smooth as possible. Recognize the importance of shared holidays and special times with his biological family members.

How Can the Church Minister to Blended Families?

Reports indicate that one-third to one-half of all Americans belong to stepfamilies.[10] Churches must meet the needs of this ever-growing population if they seek to truly meet the needs of their communities. Children of blended families can benefit from the stability of loving, caring adults at church who know them my name and care about their everyday lives. Church media libraries should make every effort to provide timely, relevant books and videos to give encouragement, strength, and guidance to families seeking to create a family unit that honors God.

Christian counselors who are staff members trained in family counseling, or staff members who devote their time to counseling ministries should be available to assist families as they seek to live together in harmony with each other and with God, giving wise counsel shaped upon the Word of God.

Blended families need opportunities to be served and to use their gifts in service as a part of the family of God. Churches should provide a loving, nonjudgmental place of refuge for families looking for a place of strength and stability during times of change.

Application and Reflection

1. Do you have personal gifts and abilities that you could use in and through your church to minister to preschoolers of blended families?

2. We often tell children that they need an attitude check. Do you or leaders in your church need an attitude check in regard to nonjudgmental ministry to blended families as they seek to become a part of your church family? Are they allowed, even encouraged, to use their God-given gifts to benefit the body of Christ?

3. Think of a blended family that you know personally and come in contact with regularly. Are you willing to commit yourself to praying daily for this family? As your relationship with this family grows, you may feel free to share with them regularly, requesting specific prayer requests on behalf of family members.

Moving

When we consider that one out of five families move every year, it is quite likely that the issues of moving will relate to your family as well. The atmosphere of a move is somewhat dictated by the reason for the move. If the move is a result of a divorce, death, or job loss, the emotions would be quite different from a move precipitated by a job promotion or a move back home closer to extended family. Regardless of the reason for a move, it will always be accompanied with a certain degree of grief. There will always be emotions tied to leaving a place where you have built memories and people whom you have loved.

The physical and emotional challenges of a move can cause added stress to a family. As the family tires physically from the labor of packing and cleaning, the disorder drains them emotionally. The combination of grief and excitement over a move can cause emotional highs and lows for family members. Great care should be given to the needs of preschoolers as families anticipate a move.

Mike Yorkey in *The Christian Family Answer Book* acknowledges three stages that are generally a part of the child's transition process. The first stage is denial. In this stage the child may announce emphatically that "he is not going. He will stay and live with a friend." In the second stage he will express anger. Most questions will begin with the word *why*. "Why did you take that job? Why are you doing this to me?" In the third stage of acceptance and adjustment the child begins to accept that the move is a reality of life and begin to find ways to adjust and begin a new life in a new place.[11]

As you prepare for the move, include children in as many

plans as possible. Explain clearly to the children why the move is necessary. Where possible, include them in the search for a new house or apartment. Note if other children are close by to play with. Take notice of homes with swing sets and riding toys that might be homes of new playmates for your child. If distance makes that impossible, provide them with pictures of the new home and neighborhood. Acquaint them with fun things they will be able to do in the area, such as zoos and amusement parks. Encourage them to share these with their friends.

Take time to read age-appropriate books on moving. Ask your church or local public media specialist to make recommendations. Allow time for talking about feelings. Talk about things you can look forward to at the new home, such as a tree swing in the backyard or at a nearby park. Accept any feelings the preschooler may express concerning the move. As much as possible, allow the preschooler to follow his normal routine.

As you prepare for moving day, plan time for final visits to favorite places and to spend time with friends and family. You might take pictures of your favorite things and favorite places and compile into a scrapbook of special memories of the old home. Encourage your child to exchange addresses and telephone numbers with special friends. A phone call to a special friend can brighten a difficult day and provide a sense of security following the move.

Preschoolers may show great excitement over an impending move, though not fully understanding what it means. Often they do not understand distance, or the fact that they will be moving but that their friends and extended family will stay behind. They have difficulty understanding packing their loved objects on a large truck for strangers to drive away. Parents should involve preschoolers in the packing process and explain the reasons for each step along the way. Be aware that one of a preschooler's greatest fears is of being left behind. Great care should be taken that favorite security objects are not packed away. In spite of the busyness of life, parents should spend quality time with the child giving reassurance as needed and maintaining a sense of stability and security for the child.

Some preschoolers may return to old, babyish behavior patterns that will soon adjust themselves. According to research, some adults and children take as long as 16 months to adjust following a move. Some families find that the weeks immediately preceding and following the move are busy and hectic, filled with a sense of excitement. It is later that reality begins to sink in and emotions of loneliness, anger, and frustration are common. Be patient and be available to help your child through this time of adjustment.

Clark Moustakas suggests in *Basic Types of Pastoral Care and Counseling* that there be a particular place or corner in the child's room for do-it-yourself play therapy methods. "This corner should be stocked with a variety of play materials such as paints and paper; puppets or doll families for fantasy play; clay for making and squashing things; a pan of water and a sand tray for messing; toys for encouraging constructive release of pent-up frustration, anger, and aggressiveness—e.g., pounding boards, punching devices and things for throwing without hurting."[12] In this area the child is able to do anything that does not hurt himself or destroy property. This type of play therapy gives the child the opportunity to play out negative feelings without causing harm to himself or others. Adults should be available to listen and respond warmly to the child when invited.

When given the proper attention and care, a move can be a positive growth experience for your child, giving her opportunities to develop new interpersonal skills and broadening knowledge and understanding of the world. A successful moving experience can result in a child with increased self-confidence.

How Can the Church Family Minister to Preschoolers and Their Families in the Midst of a Move?

Richard Shahan in *Good News for Preschoolers* suggests that during the weeks prior to the move, preschool leaders take pictures of the child with his friends involved in activities at Sunday school. Leaders could prepare a small photo album and deliver it to the child prior to the move. Leaders of church organizations might work together to prepare the album as a lasting record of special times at church. He also suggests that children make cards to be sent to the child's new address the week of the move. What joy for the child to find mail from special friends waiting for him at the new home.[13]

Application and Reflection

1. Think back to a move that you have made. Make a list of ministries that could have been helpful to you and your family.

2. Can you think of a new family in your church or neighborhood? Explore ways that you could assist the family in transition to your community.

3. Take a walk through your church facilities. Try to look as if you were seeing your church for the very first time—as through the eyes of a visiting family. What do you see? Do you see a facility that says "We value children—you are welcome here"?

Adoption

"The primary purpose of adoption is to provide a permanent family for children who cannot be cared for by their own biological parents. Therefore, the child's welfare, her needs, and her interests are the basic determinants of good adoption practice. Homes should be selected for children, rather than children selected for homes."[14]

Children needing adoptive homes come primarily from these three groups: healthy infants, special needs children, children adopted from foreign countries. Christian parents in your church may be burdened with a need to adopt those who are not easily placed. The degree of support that can be expected from the church might determine the ability of a family to reach out to children in great need of love and care.

Parents of adopted children face the questions of whether, when, and how to tell their child that he or she is adopted. Though there are different views, many feel that conversation about adoption should begin early in the relationship. It is important that the child hear this information from the parents. A child who first learns of his adoption through friends or family may feel anger or mistrust toward the parents and wonder what else they have lied about. The child may feel that the adoption was kept secret because it was considered bad or shameful.

Many experts feel that the basic foundation of telling should begin early and continue as in building blocks. Though the child has basic knowledge early, the understanding and comprehension may not come until much later. You may find yourself explaining the adoption to a preschooler and then needing to explain it all again to an eight-year-old because he was not able to understand the explanation as a preschooler. It is most important that the child be told about his adoption in a warm, loving, nurturing environment.

If you decide to tell your preschooler about adoption, remember that they only need the simplest of explanations. Your main objective is to let the preschooler know that he was very much wanted by your family. Focus on your feelings of joy and excitement upon hearing that he was coming to be a part of your family. You may share pictures of your early days together.

Adoption can be discussed as you look together through family photo albums and family videos and by reading together some of the excellent books that are available. Books such as *Let's Talk About It: Adoption* by Fred Rogers (Putnam), *I Have a New Family Now* by Robin Prince Monroe (CPH), and *How I Was Adopted* by Joanna Cole (Morrow Junior Books) are readily available in bookstores and libraries.

Though many feel it is important for children to be told of their adoption, they also feel that it should not be a constant subject. Children need to feel they are as much a part of the family as birth children. Just as you would not introduce a child as your short, red-headed daughter, you would not want to introduce a child as your adopted daughter. She is your daughter, plain and simple.

What should you tell your child about the birthparents? In spite of the fantasy figures that preschoolers may imagine, the reality is that most birthparents are regular, normal people. Regardless of their ages, their problems, their income, the bottom line is that they could not parent the child. Though the birthmother may have truly loved the child, the bottom line was she could not parent the child. Though she may have been a warm and caring person, whether she was rich or poor, she could not parent the child. Above all else, the reason for placing the child for adoption was her inability to parent the child.

The child most importantly needs to understand that regardless of the circumstances of the adoption, it was not the child's fault. Many feel that they were adopted because they were a bad child, or just not good enough for the mother to keep. In keeping with the belief that God has a master plan for our lives, stress to the child that God sent him to you. God sends some children to their parents through birth and He sends some to their parents through adoption. Allow children to hear you thanking your heavenly Father for the precious gifts He has given as He has given you children to bless your lives.

How Can the Church Bless the Lives of the Adopted?

Treasure the children that God has placed into the care of your congregation whether through birth or through adoption. Celebrate the distinct gifts that each brings to the body of Christ. Provide resources concerning adoption through your church media library for parents and for the children. Churches will want to celebrate the announcement of the adoption of a child in the same ways it celebrates the birth of a baby born into the congregation. Depending upon the age of the preschooler, those celebrations may be in the form of baby showers, a flower in their honor, a gift Bible and/or a parent-child dedication service.

Churches should be prepared to provide special ministry for preschoolers with special needs or to help with the assimilation of children who may have been adopted from other countries. Provide leadership and resources as needed to meet any special needs of the preschoolers and their parents. Especially in cases where special needs children have been adopted, parents may need additional support to care for the physical and emotional needs of the children.

"The model of family that Jesus endorses is the adoptive family. The last act of Jesus' earthly ministry recorded in the Gospel of John enacts that adoptive mode. Jesus turned the watery bonds of friendship into the blood-like bonds of kinship in the charges given to his own mother and the beloved disciple 'Woman, behold, your son!' Then he said to the disciple, 'Behold your mother.' The church follows Christ by ensuring that no one in the family of faith is family-less—that everyone is adopted into the family."[15]

Application and Reflection

1. Is your church spiritually ready and physically prepared to ensure that every child who comes into the family of faith is adopted into the family? What areas need to be strengthened in order for this to happen?

2. Does your church offer special ministries for children who have special needs? Are your facilities accessible to those who may be in wheelchairs or who may have difficulty with stairs? Are there people in your church who have special gifts and/or training in meeting special needs of children?

About the Writer

Susan Allen is Minister to Children at First Baptist Church, Statesboro, Georgia.

Notes

[1]Scripture taken from the NEW AMERICAN STANDARD BIBLE®, © Copyright The Lockman Foundation 1960, 1962, 1963, 1968, 1971, 1972, 1973, 1975, 1977. Used by permission.

[2]Gary Sprague, "The 10 Most-Asked Questions About Split-Family Ministry," *Children's Ministry Magazine*, July/August 1994.

[3]David Elkind, *The Hurried Child* (Reading MA: Addison Wesley Publishing Co., Inc., 1988), 152.

[4]Karl Zinsmeister, "Divorce's Toll on Children." *Current*, no. 390. February. 1997, 29–33.

[5]Facts for Families, Fact No. 1 (Updated 8/98), "Children and Divorce," American Academy of Child and Adolescent Psychiatry, http://www.aacap.org/factsfam/divorce.htm.

[6]Sprague, "The 10 Most-Asked Questions About Split-Family Ministry."

[7]Neil Wiseman, *It Takes a Church* (Nashville, TN: Thomas Nelson Publishers, 1996), 9.

[8]William G. Enright. "The Family Is Bigger Than You Think," *Saturday Evening Post*, May 1996, 30–32.

[9]Kevin Leman, *Living in a Stepfamily Without Getting Stepped On* (Nashville, TN: Thomas Nelson Publishers, 1994). Cited online at http://www.cyberparent.com/step/introduction.htm.

[10]"Building Kinship." CyberParent,
http://www.cyberparent.com/step/buildkin/htm.

[11]Mike Yorkey, *The Christian Family Answer Book* (Wheaton, IL: Victor Books, 1996), 178.

[12]Howard Clinebell, *Basic Types of Pastoral Care and Counseling* (Nashville, TN: Abingdon Press, 1992), 302.

[13]Richard Shahan, *Good News for Preschoolers* (Nashville, TN: Convention Press, 1998), 33.

[14]Albert Kadushin, Judith A. Martin, *Child Welfare Services* (New York: McMillan Publishing Co., 1988), 533.

[15]Diana Garland, "What Is Family Ministry?" *Christian Century* November 13, 1996, 1100–1101.

Other References

• Elizabeth Woolever, *Your Child Living With Divorce* (Des Moines, IA: Meredith Corporation, 1990).

• Scott J. South, Kyle D. Crowder, Katherine Trent, "Children's residential mobility and neighborhood environment following parental divorce and remarriage." *Social Forces*, 77, no. 2, December 1998, 667–683.

Chapter 7

Young Children During Times of War

By Bruce D. Perry

C hildren who are seeing images related to war on the news are asking a lot of questions. Teachers can help deal with these questions in several ways. Give clear and accurate answers. All people, including children, find it easier to deal with the known rather than the unknown. It is very important, however, not to drown our children in the nonstop speculation and discussion that will be provided by the media.

On the other hand, some children are not asking questions but seem to be more tense and anxious than they had been before this crisis. Are there other signs to look for that suggest "war worry" in children? Should teachers ask if war worries them and discuss the world situation further?

The symptoms that a child may exhibit when anxious will vary depending upon the individual child. Each of us has a unique style of reacting to distress. In general, if you see a child begin to behave differently, you might want to keep an eye on him. Some specific symptoms include more irritability, difficulties in concentration, or preoccupation with themes related to power, control, and safety. Some children may regress and manifest behaviors that you have not seen in years—such as regression in toileting habits or tantrums. Even if you sit down and talk with the child, do not be surprised if he minimizes any fears or acts as if he doesn't have any concerns. Often children become anxious and are unaware of why. Don't worry if they can't tell you. Reassure them that they are safe and that anytime they want to talk about things that upset them to come to you. Don't have long discussions about "the war"—they will get little from this. Just invite them to talk if they want to.

Playing with Toy Weapons

During time of war, we often see children engaging in more gun and swordplay. Increased play with weapons is not surprising at a time when the general atmosphere for a child is increasingly alarming. The most dominant images and techniques for "protection" and safety that our children have been exposed to come from the pervasive media images of guns, martial arts, swords, and other weapons that are used to defend and protect. The recent success of *Star Wars, The Lord of the Rings, Spider-Man*, and so many other high-profile "hero" stories means that our children will model these images. The choice to discourage or take away play weapons is somewhat personal. In cases where a child cannot regulate his use of these toys, or when he uses them in inappropriate ways, limiting access would be a reasonable choice.

Use of toy guns and swordplay does not need to take place in school. Physical play can be encouraged in the context of gross-motor activities. When this comes up during free play, recess, or less structured time, re-direct the play to be less aggressive.

Some teachers tell us that they see renewed interest in Ninja and other superhero figures. As children play with these figures, they often talk about how they "keep us safe." Again, this is not surprising. Fantasy play in an atmosphere of unpredictability or fear will have more use of "hero" and "heroine" characters. Books, films, toys, and art that depict these will be more compelling to young children. This is not unhealthy in moderation. Children are powerless. It helps them feel safer when they create temporary, but fantasy, worlds where they have control and power. The key is moderation.

In school, this may be an opportunity to talk about how real people faced overwhelming situations and prevailed. Bring true heroes and heroines into discussions to illustrate the alternative and productive ways in which courage, persistence, patience, words, and non-violent actions led to "victory." The more we expose our children to problem-solving behaviors other than violence, the more likely they are to see that the best solutions come from forming relationships and alliances, from persuasion and understanding—not intolerance, fear, attacking, and conquering.

Children Are Emotional Barometers

Teachers tell us that they are seeing more negative and challenging behaviors than usual, even among children who have never behaved this way. As hard as we try, sometimes our own anxieties come across one way or another. Children sense this. Children are emotional barometers. If the adults in a child's life are anxious, preoccupied, or distressed, the child may perceive this. And, of course, a child's behavior will change when he feels this persistent, low-level alarm. The most typical response it to "regress." Indeed, when anyone—adult or child—feels anxious and threatened, he thinks and acts in a less mature fashion. This means the anxious child will be more difficult to teach and parent. Remember that the world our children live in is small—home, school, and neighborhood. We have much more control, and create a safer world for children, than is possible in our larger world. In the long run, it will help children better adapt and be more productive and creative if we keep their small world safe, consistent, predictable, and nurturing. And that sense of safety comes from us.

When a teacher maintains a consistent and supportive environment in the classroom, it allows children to feel safe. If you hear a child talk about war or Iraq or Saddam Hussein, try to get her to tell you what she thinks. You will be surprised. Even very young children are likely to have overheard parents or the media discussing war. Yet they have very little understanding of what this means. It is more likely that they have many inaccurate ideas—which, in turn, may be the source of unrealistic fears.

Young children will not understand the distance to Iraq or the kind of threat it poses to their immediate neighborhood.

They may mix up recent terrorist alerts with the mobilization news and have a variety of distorted ideas. When the opportunity arises, try to give clear and accurate information.

Application and Reflection

1. What signs have your preschoolers or children shown that indicate they have become more anxious than usual about war?

2. What are the questions your young children ask about war? Write down each question and take time to think of how you might answer it. Write your response below.

3. What toys are in your home or classroom that could possibly encourage violent play?

4. How will you encourage your child not to use these toys and help him learn ways to resolve conflicts without the use of violence?

5. How can you as a parent maintain a consistent and supportive environment at home?

6. How can you do this as a teacher in your classroom? Why do you think it's important for young children to have a consistent and supportive environment?

7. What ways can you further protect your children and keep them safe?

About the Writer

Bruce D. Perry, M.D., Ph.D., is an internationally recognized authority on brain development and children in crisis. Dr. Perry leads the ChildTrauma Academy, a pioneering center providing service, research, and training in the area of child maltreatment (www.ChildTrauma.org). He is the Medical Director for Provincial Programs in Children's Mental Health for Alberta, Canada. This chapter was adapted from an article in *Early Childhood Today* magazine (April 2003). Used by permission.

Chapter 8

Working with the Child Who Has Post-Traumatic Stress Disorder

By Stanley I. Greenspan

Apreschool teacher was concerned about a 4-year-old in her class. A house fire caused the family to have to re-locate, and the child lost many of his toys and other personal possessions. "I find myself," the teacher said, "con-stantly on the alert for any signs he might show of post-trau-matic stress disorder (PTSD). Are there specific things I should look for? And if I notice these signs, what should I do about them?"

Signs of having been exposed to severe stress or having ex-perienced trauma vary from child to child. What we look for is any change in the child's usual functioning. Tummy aches and sleep problems are additional stress signals as are increased fear-fulness and anxiety, and increased aggression. A child might also experience nightmares, though this is not as common as the other three reactions.

Often, there are changes in academic performance that indicate possible exposure to unusual stress. In this case, a child who had been learning with ease may all of a sudden seem to be very distracted and unable to absorb concepts very well.

Changes in Play Styles

There's a belief among many that you are likely to see reenactments of the trauma in a child's play, but you are more likely to see a change or shift in the child's *style* of play. For instance, a child who hasn't been imaginative may begin playing out chaotic, frantic scenes with toys being thrown around—but not necessarily replaying the exact type of trauma he was exposed to. Of course, some children will play out the drama that they were exposed to, the event that scared them. Sometimes they change it, and sometimes you'll see it being played out exactly as it happened. Whatever the behavior of the child, whether it's becoming more shy, more fearful, or more aggressive, it's important to address his anxieties.

Responding to Anxiety

While you have to certainly set limits on aggressive behavior, you want to be especially gentle while you're being firm. The child may already be scared and traumatized. Getting "tough" with him in a punitive way won't help him get through these scary feelings and will only tend to make him want to be more aggressive.

With the child who becomes shy, the situation is a little

easier because he's obviously frightened, and you're dealing with his feelings more directly. In both cases, whether you have a child who is clearly fearful or one who's showing anxiety in other ways, you want to do pretty much the same thing:

• Start with extra nurturing—providing a stronger sense of security.
• Don't overload him.
• Offer him a little more time with you.
• Try to pair him up with other children at activity times who are very calming, nurturing, and soothing.

Encourage the child to talk about how he's feeling, but be very gentle and not intrusive. And if the child seems to want to avoid talking about feelings, just say, "Gee, sometimes even talking can be scary." In other words, don't push it, but allude to the child's avoidance of the issue.

Try also to reassure the child, to the degree that you can, that the particular scary thing he's been exposed to won't happen again. Tell him what steps you're taking to protect him. Point out the steps others have been taking, too, including the police or the government.

Finally, help the child to be active in coping by contributing something. For example, many children have made cards for the firefighters and police officers, thanking them for being so brave on September 11th.

Throughout the process of working with post-traumatic stress, it is essential to coordinate your efforts with those of the parents. Help the parents to follow the same steps described here, and continue to stay in touch and compare notes.

Application and Reflection

1. Write down the names of young children you might know who suffer from post-traumatic stress syndrome. Underneath each child's name, write what signs of the syndrome you have noticed. How will you respond to this particular child?

2. What ways will you as a teacher work with the parents of these children listed above? If you are a parent, how will you seek help from your child's teacher? For each family, design a plan of action to work toward to help that particular child. Include what parents can do and what teachers can do to help. Keep track of each child's progress and make appropriate reports to either the teacher or parent. What would you do in addition to the list suggested in the chapter?

3. Spend time praying daily for families in your care. If you are a parent, pray for your child's teacher as well as your own family.

About the Writer

Stanley I. Greenspan, M.D., is co-author, with T. Berry Brazelton, M.D., of *The Irreducible Needs of Children* (Perseus Press, 2000). Dr. Greenspan is a clinical professor of psychiatry, behavioral science, and pediatrics at the George Washington University Medical School. This chapter was adapted from an article in *Early Childhood Today* magazine (March 2002). Used by permission.

Resources for Parents and Teachers

- *Building Healthy Minds* by Stanley I. Greenspan, M.D., and Nancy Breslau Lewis (Perseus Press, 2000).

- *Playground Politics* by Stanley I. Greenspan, M.D. (Perseus Press, 1994).

- *The Secure Child* by Stanley I. Greenspan, M.D. (Perseus Press, 2002).

Chapter 9

Helping Young Children Cope with Terrorism

By Jim Greenman

C hildren's lives have always been marked by change. Each day brings new revelations that life is filled with storms as well as sunshine. No child ultimately escapes from the experience of fear, loss, grief, and trauma. But extraordinary events that shatter the sense of security of everyone they know and love put a particular pressure on the adults in their lives to be at their best as parents and caregivers.

The attacks of terror on a beautiful day in September 2001, and the revelations that more attacks were planned and may be expected in the future, have created a new national reality. The aftermath of a declaration of war on terror, as well as the certain increase in bomb threats, false alarms, and rumors, guarantee that life will be different for children and families for the foreseeable future.

The September 11 attacks were the act of terrorists who hated the politics of the United States. America was attacked by a terrorist organization, not a country and not an Islamic or Muslim movement. Times of conflict and war usually reduce human relationships to "us vs. them" and challenge our capacity for tolerance and understanding. We owe it to our children to resist intolerance and prejudice and to help them grow up understanding our common humanity and respecting our differences.

While this chapter is a response to the events of September 11, 2001, almost all of the insight into children's thinking and behavior and what they need from the adult world applies to other calamities, personal and social; death; natural disaster; and violence. Every day, individual children touched by life's darker side are asking: "What happened to my world?"

What Happened to the World?

On September 11, 2001, three blocks from the World Trade Center, a little girl left her child care center with her teacher to reunite with her mother. Stepping out onto the sidewalk, as her eyes, ears, and nose took in the gray air and ankle-deep debris, the amazed child exclaimed for all of us, "What happened to the world?" The teacher could offer no answer other than, "You're safe with us. Let's go find your mom." And that is just what they did.

What are we to answer?

The events of that day touched everyone. Certainly the millions in New York, Washington, D.C., and Pennsylvania who experienced the blast and the aftermath know firsthand the trauma. Anyone who commutes to those cities, who travels by air, who works in a tall building or a federal building, who visits New York or Washington, or knows someone who does, is also affected. And, as the fear of further acts of terrorism grows, anyone who can say, "That could have been me or someone I love" is joined by many others who will worry, "That could be me or someone I love—next time."

When will life return to normal? Almost certainly, never. The country and its families will construct a new idea of normal so that life can go on and we can rebuild. We live in a 24-hour instant news culture where dramatic images of horror or grief surround our children. The "new normal" for children will have to be a world where they come to terms with a new sense of threat and possible conflict, but nonetheless have the internal resources and support to live happy, productive lives.

The child's world today is a global village, and children will have to understand what it means to live with others who look and sound different, have different cultures and values, and practice different religions. They live here and in faraway lands. In the September 11 disaster, more than 5000 people from 80 countries perished. News of all the events was instantly broadcast worldwide, and the search for friends and enemies was a global one. If our lives and the lives of our children are not to be shrouded in conflict, we will need to learn understanding, tolerance, and respect for others—a difficult task when the drumbeat of conflict creates a "for us or against us" mentality.

A climate of terrorism and war touches us all, but not equally. Some will experience much more pain and distress. In addition to those who have or will experience the events directly, there are many others already living with trauma or overwhelming stress who are vulnerable to new blows. There are also children and adults whose high sensitivity to tragedy and trauma leaves them particularly vulnerable in times when fear and tragedy are ever-present.

What's happened to the world? It has become a place where we need to support each other and our children more than ever before.

Children Need Our Strength

Adults largely set the emotional landscape for children. Children depend on us to be strong and solid, to know what is happening, and to guide them through the shoals of troubled waters.

How are you feeling now in a world proclaimed to be at war with terrorism, and what might that mean today or tomorrow? Knowing how you feel and finding your way to higher ground is critical to helping the children you love and care for. Even as babies, children see, hear, and feel our pain and despair, and they look to us for understanding, reassurance, and hope. They have a sixth sense that detects unease and uncertainty. When disaster strikes, every child wants to know from you:

Will I be okay?

Will you be okay?

Will everybody I care about be okay?

The first step in helping children cope with turbulent times is to sort through our own feelings and get the support we need. Children need from us all the love, strength, reassurance, and calm we can muster. Their sense of safety stems from us.

One distraught mother said: "I tried to keep talking with my children about what happened on September 11, and they just didn't seem to care—only that their TV shows were off. My husband is a pastor, and last night we organized a silent candlelight walk down the main streets of our town. The thing my son was excited about was that HE got to carry the flag. This seemed important to him only because it was fun. I have four children between the ages of 6 and 15 years old. Even my most sensitive child seems not to care. What can I do to help them understand the magnitude of what has happened? I thought maybe they were not talking because they were so scared…but they said they were not scared. I asked them what they thought. They decided that we should just annihilate the enemy. (Unfortunately, they got that idea from me.) I talked about the children who will be coming home to a missing parent. I asked them how they would feel if one day Dad just went off to work as usual and never came home again. I just can't get through to them. Please help me."

The anguished parent's emotional reaction probably overwhelmed her children. Their reaction to the catastrophe and the distress at home was actually fairly normal. Some experienced the attacks of terror themselves or through the life of someone they knew. But many more watched the television, thinking, "That could have been me or my friend or relative. We could be next. Why them and not us?"

We all feel and behave differently in response to trauma; the timing and intensity of our feelings and the behavior changes that follow vary from person to person. Some take it all in in a great rush and open wound of emotion; others compartmentalize or push feelings down and try to manage the response. The stress in each of our lives varies widely, as do the supports that we have to cushion and offset the large and small challenges to our well being. But somewhere inside, we all feel frightened and vulnerable.

Common Emotional Reactions to Trauma

- **Shock:** How could this happen?
- **Confusion:** What does it all mean?
- **Fear or worry:** What will happen next; where, when, and to whom? Will it end?
- **Grief** for someone I loved, or someone else like me or those whom I love.
- **Anger** at the people who perpetrated the attacks, at the cruelty and unfairness of it all.
- **Guilt:** Why them and not me? It's not like me to hate and want revenge.
- **Helplessness:** I can't make my world like it was—a safe, manageable place.
- **Sadness:** Lives lost, children orphaned, futures turned to dust and ash.
- **Isolation or alienation:** I'm not sure if anyone understands my feelings.
- **Hopelessness:** I'm not sure all this effort is worth it; what does it matter?

Common Changes in Behavior

- Appetite changes
- Change in sleeping patterns
- Anxiety
- Tension
- Headaches and low resistance to illness
- Crying
- Anger or short temper
- Fatigue
- Hyperactivity
- Mood swings
- Difficulty concentrating
- Numbness or apathy
- Depression

All of these reactions are normal, up to a point. You are not alone in these responses. But when the reaction is intense and prolonged, seeking help is important for you and the children for whom you care.

To take care of children, you need to take care of yourself. Here are some suggestions:

- Talk about your feelings with adults with whom you feel secure.
- Try to create a daily routine and rituals that support your current needs (routine is a morning cup of coffee; ritual is more personal—drinking the coffee from your favorite cup while sitting in a chair by the window.)
- Try to create a daily routine and rituals that support your family's current needs.
- Live well: eat right, get exercise, sleep.

- Cry when you need to, and seek solitude when you have to.
- Take breaks from the news and the headlines.
- Take breaks from others who bring you down.
- Give yourself and those around you some slack for poor behavior under stress.
- Seek help if you feel that life is not becoming more manageable.
- Replenish your spirit with friends, faith, family, music, and nature.

Understanding and Supporting Children

A week after the terror in New York, 4-year-old Kia asked her mom when the planes would stop crashing and the buildings stop falling. Her mother reassured her that it was all over. "No, Mom, it happened again last night, and this morning," said Kia. "Come look!" Kia insisted, and her mother once again saw the familiar images appearing on the TV screen.

"But that's the same plane and the same building. That happened last week," her mother explained.

"Oh," said Kia, still convinced that hundreds of planes had attacked hundreds of buildings.

The planes keep crashing into the buildings. The buildings keep falling down. The people keep emerging covered with dust and blood, day after day. And if you are a child watching the news, it doesn't stop. If you happen to be 3 or 4 or 5 years old, still learning to navigate the confusing borders of time and space and what is real and what isn't, you probably think it's dozens of planes and dozens of buildings. The child may be thinking, "When will it happen to me?"

Every child is different. Anne, at the age of 3, paid close attention to TV reports of any threat—crime, hurricanes, and earthquakes—and nightmares always followed. The loss of a pet, a friend moving away, and the sorrows of distant others were all felt intensely. Alejandro, on the other hand, breezed through his childhood with only a brief pause for the real calamities that occurred around him. Kim's vivid imagination and her empathy for others left her seriously vulnerable when any tragedy crossed her path. Malik and Tyler's 9-year-old responses to airplane crashes were similar: while not appearing particularly upset, each needed precise answers on an infinite number of details about the crash. And 15-year-old Steven never let on that anything would shake his cool veneer.

Obviously, children are different, from adults and from each other. But remembering that in practice is not always easy for parents and teachers. Children think very differently from adults, and at each stage of development, they view the world through their own unique lenses.

All children are vulnerable, but not equally. A child already grieving over a lost loved one (including a pet), divorce, or separation, may feel more vulnerable, as will children who have families in crisis, or who are under stress for any number of reasons. Unusually sensitive and empathetic children will also struggle more to come to terms with events.

Supporting children during times of uncertainty and stress begins with knowing your child. The best indicators of distress in children are *changes* in their behavior. Watch for behavior that is not typical for the child: a normally outgoing child behaving shyly or withdrawing; or a child becoming whiny, irritable, or anger-prone. A child may regress to past behavior, thumb sucking or defiance, clinging, or not showing the self-help skills of which he or she is capable.

Remember, not all behaviors or behavior changes stem from a crisis. All the other aspects of life and development are marching on—adjusting to a new school, friends moving away, parents worried about layoffs—all create personal stress that may eclipse societal turmoil.

Preschool Children

They know more than you think, and much of it is incomplete or misconceived. Preschool children are much more aware of world events than we think, but their understanding is limited. Very young children are magical thinkers and do not live in our adult world. They confuse fantasy and reality, time and space, and are working through the concepts of cause and effect and permanence. Their daily world is already populated with monsters, disasters, nightmares, and heroes. The images on the news are not different from the fictional images they see on the television screen, so the major impact of the terror and its aftermath is the effect that it has on adults: new fears of bombs; anxiety about air travel, buildings falling down, and the threat of war. Children pay attention to adult words, and words such as *attack*, *revenge*, and *retaliation* may make them feel insecure. Preschool children have a conscious awareness that people can come and go, and in times of crisis are likely to have fears of abandonment. They feel helpless because they now understand that they need protection and care, and they worry, "Something might happen to those I love and need."

Children's sensitivity to tragic events as depicted on television varies widely. Some children barely notice or shake it off relatively quickly; some are very traumatized. Most children fall in between those poles. Preschool children may ask a lot of questions. They need honest answers, but do not need details that will disturb them. Do not bring up issues that don't appear to be on the child's mind, but do listen for hidden questions. Remember the old story about the 5-year-old who asked, "Where did I come from?" Following a short discussion of where babies come from, the child said, "Okay, but Tony came from Iowa. What about me?"

Play is how children make sense of and come to terms with a world that offers surprises and puzzles every day. Play is how children achieve mastery over the situations in which they are powerless. Their dramatic play may reflect current events:

- Building and destroying block towers
- Flying and crashing planes
- Playing police officers or soldiers
- Playing doctors, rescue workers, and the injured or the dead

Preschool children also use art to work through and express thoughts and feelings.

They need adults who recognize that playing through life's horrors is normal, who listen to them, and who do not react harshly, preach, or condemn. Children need to play at being powerful, even at being "bad guys." Unless play might lead to a child becoming hurt physically or emotionally, it is usually best not to intervene.

Common Preschool Reactions to Stress
- Bed-wetting
- Fear of the dark, monsters, or animals
- Clinging to parents and caregivers
- Nightmares
- Toileting accidents—loss of bladder or bowel control, constipation
- Speech difficulties (a loss for words, stammering)
- Loss or increase of appetite
- Cries or screams for help
- Fear of being left alone; fear of strangers
- Confusion
- Testing behavior

These can all be normal preschool behaviors. The key is to look for changes in a particular child's behavior.

What Do Children Under Age 5 Need?
- Normal routines and favorite rituals
- A peaceful household
- Limited exposure to media and adult conversations about the crisis
- Ample time with calm, loving, reassuring adults
- Much verbal reassurance that you and they will be okay
- Plenty of physical reassurance (hugs, snuggling)
- To know where you and the others they love are at any given time
- Opportunities for you to listen and gentle conversation
- Opportunities to draw or use clay to express themselves
- Opportunities for and acceptance of play that may reflect

the current events with intervention only to avoid harm
- Special time and reassurance at bedtime, including letting the child sleep with you

Questions About Terrorism and War

How do we answer younger children's questions about terrorism? As Fred Rogers said: "There are some people in this world who are very angry and haven't learned how to live with people they don't agree with." They come in all colors and live in different places. And sometimes they do terrible, awful things to hurt people. But there are many more people who know how to get along, and they are all over the world, working hard to stop these people who do terrible things.

How do we answer younger children's questions about war? Keep it simple: "Sometimes whole countries, after much talking, still can't decide about how to get along. They have armies that fight each other. Or army is very strong and works hard to make sure that we are all safe."

Studies show that boys are fascinated with implements of action and power, particularly weapons. It is important to accept that many boys will be fascinated by and drawn to warlike behavior: both attacking and defending. For younger children, rather than quickly banishing or condemning warlike play, recognize that police cars, ambulances, rescue helicopters, planes, boats, cranes, and trucks are also equally dramatic implements of action and power that help and rescue. Of course, girls will also be drawn to dramatic action play.

What do we tell children whose loved ones face military service? Again, children need honesty and reassurance appropriate for their developmental level. If mom or a big sister is in the military: "She has a job to do and is trained to do that job. We are all a little scared and will miss her a lot when she is gone—and she is really going to miss us too." It can help to involve the child in keeping the one she loves safe and connected. "We will pray for her every day and write postcards to her, draw pictures for her, keep a journal, and make a book of her letters. We can put markers on a map and trace her journeys."

Children's Exposure to Death

Terrorist attacks and the fact of war bring the reality and idea of death to the foreground of children's lives. To young children, death is another "magical" part of life. If someone who cares for them dies, they often feel abandoned. Because they believe the world revolves around them, they may feel it was something that they caused. Death is important to them because it is important to us; it upsets them because it upsets us. They don't understand the finality of death or the emotional weight of grieving.

Children react to how the adults in their lives react to death and dying. The personal feelings and behaviors that they witness will create a climate of security or insecurity.

Children and families who are experiencing the death of a loved one under traumatic circumstances need to draw on relatives and friends for support. They should also take advantage of the resources provided by employers, communities, and others who provide resources.

Respect for Others

Children can learn prejudice at a very young age. They can learn to fear differences, stereotype others, and reject others because of identity. They learn this from the adults and children around them and from television and movies. Intolerance of others begins with ignorance and fear. Education is crucial to our attempts to create a more peaceful world. Children need to be taught about humanity, human rights, and tolerance in order to combat images and stereotypes from the media and the world around them.

During the time following the September 11 crisis in the United States, the most vulnerable populations were the Arab-American community, Muslims, and citizens of the Middle East. Middle Eastern stereotypes already abound in television, movies, cartoons, computer games, and comic books. They are almost never portrayed as positive characters or heroes. Very little understanding is demonstrated of the cultures of the Middle East, or of the relationships between Islam, Judaism, and Christianity.

Children will express what they hear adults saying, and this gives us an opportunity. If children express fear or antagonism toward people of Middle Eastern descent, ask them to explain what they are thinking and feeling. At the child's developmental level, explain that although a few Middle Eastern people or Muslims hate American policies and did a terrible thing, many more think hurting others is terrible, and they do not hate America. There are millions and millions of Arabs and Muslim children and parents in the U.S. and around the world who were sad, confused, angry, and shocked at what happened on September 11.

Tolerance begins at home, and school and education are crucial to our attempts to create a more tolerant world. Educators and families can prevent dehumanization, prejudice, and stereotyping. Remember to watch what you say about others, because your preschoolers learn from you!

Toward a Better World

In times of crisis it is important to find strength and reassurance in our communities, our diversity, and our common commitment to learning how to develop a better world. Crises can bring into focus that we are one world, a world that our children will inherit. There is a pull toward oversimplifying issues and ideologies, friends and foes, and violence is a frequent means for expressing good and evil. Children need to be taught about the world and its diverse people, and to develop an empathy and thoughtfulness that underlies their judgment. They need to learn how to solve problems peacefully and to draw upon the strength of their family, community, nation, and the world.

Children are surrounded by heroes, in person and on the screen. In addition to the firefighters, police, rescue workers, armed forces, and all those who helped the victims or survived the devastation, there are others.

When parents and teachers give children their strength when they themselves are feeling shaken or overwhelmed with their own feelings of uncertainty, fear, or grief, they are heroes.

When parents and teachers recognize their own anger and biases, when they resist the urge to scapegoat and hate and instead teach their children tolerance and respect for others, they are heroes.

When the sky is falling, when the noise is deafening, and the darkness grows, children need all the shelter and light that we can bestow upon them.

Application and Reflection

1. What ways will you help your child accept differences in other people?

2. How will you teach your child respect for differences in culture, physical appearance, customs, etc.?

3. How will you lead your child to know that God made us all different, yet we are all alike?

4. As an adult, what are your prejudices or biases? How do you deal with these? How do you think your own prejudices affect your children?

5. Why is it important to teach your child tolerance and respect? Make a list of the ways you can do this.

6. How can your family learn to solve problems peacefully?

About the Writer

Jim Greenman is Senior Vice President of Education and Program Development for Bright Horizons Family Solutions. This chapter is excerpted from his 2001 book, *What Happened to the World? Helping Children Cope in Turbulent Times*, available from the National Association of Educators of Young Children at www.naeyc.org. Used by permission.

Resources for Parents and Teachers

Children and Trauma: A Parent Guide to Helping Children Heal, by Cynthia Monahon (Lexington Books, 1995).

Teaching Young Children in Violent Times: Building a Peaceable Classroom, by Diane Levin (Cambridge: Educators for Social Responsibility).

Remote Control Childhood: Combating the Hazards of Media Culture, by Diane Levin (Washington, DC: National Association of Educators of Young Children).

Talking with Your Child About a Troubled World, by Lynne Dumas (NY: Fawcett, 1992).

Chapter 10

Walk Through Crises Together

By Karen Dockrey

I crunched myself into position, serving as the pillow for my hunched-over daughter, Emily. Her goal was to make her back as round as possible so the spinal tap needle could enter her spine in the least painful position. She struggled to relax as a huge needle approached her back. With her body around mine, I could compliment her relaxed state or talk her into renewed calmness if she became tense.

"Un-way, oo-tay, ee-thray," counted Emily's nurse in pig Latin, to distract Emily from the painful procedure. "Ood-gay irl-gay. It's-ay ipping-dray." The needle was in, and the spinal fluid was dripping on the first try. This nurse was so skilled. She let Emily know what to expect and then did each step with speed and precision, all the while talking in pig Latin to make it easier.

The nurse gave a play-by-play to let Emily know when the first tube of spinal fluid was full ("ube-tay un-way"), the second ("ube-tay oo-tay"), and finally the third ("ube-tay ee-thray"). Those three minutes seemed like an eternity. "Ime-tay or-fay the edicine-may," said the nurse to let Emily know she would hold the needle steady long enough to insert the medicine to replace the now-missing spinal fluid. While the fluid dripped, the needle had hung loose and didn't hurt much. Holding it steady would increase the pain. The nurse talked more during this time to help Emily manage it.

"The edicine-may is-ay in-ay. The eedle-nay is-ay oming-cay out-ay. Un-way, oo-tay, ee-thray," said the nurse as she pulled out the needle.

"You can sit up now," a relieved me told my relieved daughter. "It's over again for another week."

Together we'd made it through one more in the seemingly endless series of spinal taps, a procedure to verify that no more leukemia cells had entered Emily's central nervous system and to prevent any from going there.

You and your child walk through the crisis together. Together you can manage the pain, talk through the dread, and cope with the aftereffects.

God knows how important company is on the scary walk through pain. The Bible describes the power of God's company: "Even though I walk through the valley of the shadow of death, I will fear no evil, for you are with me; your rod and your staff, they comfort me" (Psalm 23:4).

And the Bible affirms the value of human company: "Two are better than one…If one falls down, his friend can help him up.…if two lie down together, they will keep warm. But how can one keep warm alone? Though one may be overpowered, two can defend themselves. A cord of three strands is not quickly broken" (Ecclesiastes 4:9–12).

You Can Run But You Can't Hide

Like our children, we'd like to put off the shot, the stitches, and the painful encounter until another day. But what has to be done has got to be done. All the wishes in the world won't make the bone heal without proper setting and casting. All your anger that your child has to go through continuing pain won't prevent your diabetic child from needing a daily insulin injection. All your fear of needles won't complete the biopsy. Rather than abandon your child to face painful procedures alone, empower your child with your presence. Overcome your own pain by focusing on your child.

Walk through the crisis together, recognizing pain as something you go through, not something you end with. Perhaps that's the first key to managing pain—knowing there's joy on the other side. Some of this joy comes naturally: the joy of the procedure being over, the joy of going back home, the joy of the next activity. You may want to provide other joy yourself: dance a silly jig after each day's insulin shot, decorate the new cast with glow-in-the-dark markers, or meet Dad for lunch after the tedious hearing test. When circumstances permit, talk with your child about what he'd like to do after the hurting is over. Then focus on that joy as you walk through the crisis.

A Child's Viewpoint

Children see painful and scary procedures as exactly that—painful and scary. They don't care whether the shot will help them or not. They don't want it because it hurts. Rather than respond with logic, give comfort and presence. Of course, you'll explain that the purpose of the procedure is to help your child get better, but focus on helping him through the experience.

Let's face it. A shot is a shot. Anything with needles is going to hurt. But it can hurt less. There are four basic ways to reduce pain:

- EMLA
- Speed
- Distraction
- A skillful nurse or doctor

Pray for and seek health-care givers who work well with your child and who do painful procedures quickly, effectively, and relatively painlessly. If your child faces repeated procedures, notice professionals who worked well before and request them next time. This is not the time to defer to medical training needs; instead, kindly but firmly request the person your child most trusts and the one who is best at the procedure. Then together with your health-care practitioner, try one or more of these approaches to speed up the process or distract your child from the pain.

- Apply EMLA to the site of the injection, biopsy, spinal tap, or other procedure. This by-prescription-only cream numbs the site so completely that pain is almost eliminated for many procedures. The cream must be applied an hour or more in advance. Insist on this no matter how old your child is or how "simple" the injection. There's no reason to endure unnecessary pain.

• Tell your child about the procedure early enough to let him get ready, but not early enough to prompt undue worry. Some children like to know several hours ahead; others prefer a ten-second warning. My Emily does not want to know the date of her chemotherapy appointment or the procedures that await her until she wakens that day.

• Once your child knows the shot or other painful procedure is coming, do it quickly.

• Hold your child in your lap, put your arms around him, or touch him in whatever way he finds comforting. Whisper calming words.

• Give your child as much control as possible by allowing her to say "3-2-1-go" or by letting her choose where on the table to sit. While allowing the child to count to three, don't let her delay the procedure through telling one more story, asking to count higher, or running to the restroom. Sometimes the anticipation really is worse than the procedure.

• Teach your child how to relax his body through deep breathing or other relaxation techniques. Let him breathe rapidly to cope with intense parts of the process. These effective-for-childbirth techniques also work for other pain. The key is knowing how to breathe when. Your nurse will help you and your child know.

- Give your child a pinwheel and challenge her to blow it as fast as it will go. She will pay more attention to this activity than to the shot or procedure.

- Talk through the procedure in pig Latin (ig-pay atin-lay) or other silly language. Translating the instructions distracts from the pain.

- Take along a wrapped gift to open after the procedure. Squeezing and guessing the gift can both distract your child and make her want to complete the procedure. Rattly, soft, or squeezable presents are especially effective. For continuing crises, keep a box of wrapped gifts and let your child choose one before leaving home. Let friends who ask, "What can I do?" fill this present box.

- During an extended procedure, talk with your child about something he likes. If your son fishes, invite him to tell the nurse about his last fishing trip—what color the water was, how many fish he caught, what the fish looked like, and more. As he talks, he focuses less on the pain.

- Tell stories or play a tape of yourself telling stories. Play the stories through headphones if the procedure is noisy.

- Invite your child to take along a stuffed animal or comforting blanket.

- Explain exactly what will happen if it helps your child to prepare for what's coming. This approach lets her know that it won't hurt unless you warn her first.

- Don't tell what's coming if your child prefers that. One teenager covers his head with a coat and sings a song to himself while he undergoes procedures. He does better when he doesn't know what's coming.

- Let your child play her favorite music and sing or hum along.

- Agree on a treat afterward, such as going out to a specific restaurant, baking cookies, or visiting someone special. Some call this bribery. I call it anticipating the pleasant future.

- Maintain some sense of humor about everything, letting your child take the lead and telling jokes *with* your child rather than *about* him—"Mmmm, this hospital food is the greatest. I can hardly wait to eat it."

- Ask medical professionals for unused syringes (without needles, of course), bandages, anesthesia masks, and other items used in the procedure so the child can play through the process at home. This activity helps him prepare for repeated procedures and work through feelings about a past procedure. Playing helps a child understand what has happened or will happen, express his feelings, and feel in control.

It all boils down to finding what makes your child most

comfortable and doing it. Be willing to try something you wouldn't usually do—such as sing a song out loud—to help your child relax. When possible, call ahead to learn details of the procedure, to request health-care givers who are especially good with your child's age and temperament, and to choose the least busy time of day for the procedure. Do whatever works for your child.

Children in medical crises need doctors who will talk with them and treat them as people. They need nurses who can give shots quickly and relatively painlessly with no extra sticks. Children need technicians who can attach the casts and give the x-rays with humor and a sense of adventure. Armed with both appreciation and high expectation, find the medical teams who can help your child in these ways. Children are children, not guinea pigs, not miniature adults, not "cases." Protect your children from overzealous interns and from being used as learning material for bumbling doctors. Certainly we need to cooperate with teaching hospitals, because experience with our children may save another child's life. But be certain the students are skilled in doing procedures as painlessly as possible. Be certain that promising professionals know how to diagnose and treat accurately. If you are uncertain, tactfully request that an experienced professional accompany the rookie.

Equip with Information and Encouragement

You can't always be with your child. Parents are rarely allowed in the recovery room and even less often in the operating room. You can't go to school with your child, nor can you accompany him through his private thoughts. For circumstances like these, equip your child with information, recommendations, Bible promises, and assurance.

When Lorenzo was scheduled for one-day surgery, his mom found out as much as she could about the procedure. After talking with the doctor, she called the day surgery unit at the hospital and asked to speak with someone who worked in that unit and could explain the policies.

"This is Laura Galindo. My son Lorenzo will have ear tubes inserted Thursday by Dr. Hill. Is this a good time to explain the day surgery process to me?"

"Certainly! What do you want to know?" asked a short-stay nurse.

"We want to know what will happen from the minute we walk in the hospital door until we leave. I'll explain these details to my son so he will know what's coming and will be less apprehensive," said Mrs. Galindo.

"When you first arrive, you'll fill out paperwork. Then, after waiting a short time, Lorenzo will go to a room where he'll give a urine sample and a blood sample. Tell him he can choose his own bandage and the nurses give stickers," said the nurse.

"He'll like that," said Mrs. Galindo.

"Then the two of you will go to the short-stay unit where Lorenzo will have his own room with a television and closet. I, or a member of my staff, will meet you there. You might want to bring a few things to do, because he may have to wait a while there or wait at some of the previous stops.

"While Lorenzo changes into a hospital gown, I'll ask you more questions. Then we'll take his temperature and blood pressure. About an hour before surgery we'll wheel him to the holding room. You might tell him how fun it is to ride on a rolling bed," suggested the nurse.

Mrs. Galindo thanked the nurse for knowing what would matter to her small son. She felt safe putting him in her care.

"The anesthesiologist, the surgical nurse, and perhaps the doctor will speak to you in the holding room," continued the nurse. "Following surgery your son will spend about thirty minutes in recovery and then return to you in the short-stay unit."

"How long can we stay with him?" asked Lorenzo's mom.

"You'll be with him until they take him from the holding room to surgery. Then as soon as he wakes up in recovery, we'll bring him to you," said the nurse. "All in all, he'll be away from you about an hour."

"Can he take anything with him into surgery?" asked Mrs. Galindo.

"Certainly. A blanket, a teddy bear, or something else that he likes. Be sure to let the surgical nurse know what he's taking so she can help keep up with it. Sometimes they put a bandage on the doll or teddy bear," added the nurse.

Lorenzo's mom explained these details to Lorenzo. She asked him to let her know what the anesthesia smelled like and to count the people in each room. She then assured Lorenzo that she would be waiting for him after the operation was over and that God would be taking good care of him, even when she couldn't be there.

Lorenzo returned from surgery saying, "Like bubble gum and five. The stuff smelled like bubble gum, and five people were in the last room."

The challenges gave Lorenzo something to focus on besides

fear. The information kept him from fearing the unknown. The assurance helped him know that his parent would be nearby and that God would walk with him through every step of surgery.

When You Can't Be There

Nikki faced continual ridicule at the school lunch table. Her dad wanted to march into the cafeteria and knock a couple of heads together, but he knew that wouldn't do. Besides, Nikki wanted to solve the problem herself. They took turns listing possibilities.

- Dad said Nikki could move to another lunch table, but Nikki said the other tables were full.

- Nikki wanted to skip lunch, but Dad said she needed the break, the nourishment, and the confidence that she didn't have to run from problems.

- Dad suggested Nikki try guiding the conversation by asking questions to get the girls talking about subjects that wouldn't lead to ridicule.

- Nikki thought of ridiculing back, but she didn't want to hurt them or fight fire with fire.

- Dad and Nikki generated reasons the girls said such cruel things—taking their frustrations out on her, expressing jealousy, saying what others said, not knowing what else to talk about. Nikki repeated her commitment to never hurt someone by talking the way they talked to her.

• Nikki said there were other people she'd rather sit with, but she didn't know them well enough yet.

• Dad suggested she try to make friends one by one with other people.

The two decided Nikki would do this last step and watch for open places at other tables. If she got nearer the front of the line, more places might be open. They agreed the problem was not an easy one. Dad continued to listen as Nikki poured out her hurt and anger. He told her how angry it makes him when someone hurts her. They found Matthew 10:19–20 as a reminder of God's care in the lunchroom: "But when they arrest you, do not worry about what to say or how to say it. At that time you will be given what to say, for it will not be you speaking, but the Spirit of your Father speaking through you." Nikki felt better just knowing her dad cared.

During your child's time of crisis, you can give:
  • Tools
  • Information
  • Challenges
  • Ideas
  • Assurance
  • Encouragement both when you can and when you can't be there.

You Can Run and Hide Now

When the surgery, treatment, or trauma is over, you and your child can, and probably should, hide (see Matthew 14:23). This retreat gives God an opportunity to heal and refresh you. Your hibernation period can be as brief as a deep breath or as long as a weekend getaway.

Take the time both you and your child need to rest, to heal, and to recuperate. Some parents like to rest with friends; others prefer family time. For deeply traumatic or continuing crises, some families need up to a year or more of reduced activity, mingling daily responsibilities with times for reflection. Discover the way God heals you best.

I try to approach my daughter's chemotherapy logically, reminding myself that she is doing well, that the chemo can whip the cancer once and for all, that three out of four weeks are basically free of side effects, that we can get through the chemo week because we've made it through before. But when my daughter and I return home from a day at the cancer clinic, I'm wiped out every time. This chemo visit happens on a Wednesday. On Wednesday nights I teach a youth Bible study class followed by a youth worker meeting. I've tried going on to church on these nights, but I'm too exhausted emotionally to finish my sentences or to stay patient with my active high school group. So I get a substitute ahead of time, and my family huddles together to recover. By the weekend, the chemotherapy side effects are so severe that we miss Sunday school and church, also. We go off to a motel to concentrate fully on our daughter's needs. We call these trips "adventure weekends," trying to mingle a little joy with the pain. Anticipating the joy helps my daughter—and the rest of the family—through the chemotherapy.

Here's a ministry tip: Volunteer to take over for your friend's church or work responsibilities during a crisis. You'll minister in an important way, because your friend cares deeply for the people in her class and the responsibilities at work. She wants to know they're well taken care of in her absence. Because a continuing crisis is not over in the first week or two, ask the dates of return doctor visits and restate your offer to substitute or help in another way.

The children at our pediatric cancer clinic have their own way of retreating. As each child emerges from the treatment room, the waiting room crowd applauds. Then the children start their party. They find all kinds of reasons to celebrate— birthdays, Christmas, Valentine's Day, the end of someone's chemo, cure day, unparty day. Knowing a party awaits makes going to the cancer clinic more fun and makes the aftereffects more bearable.

Helena has discovered a post-chemotherapy retreat that works uniquely for her. Her medicines make her too nauseated to party afterward, so she and a friend do something fun the night before. They stay up really late so she'll be sleepy on chemo day. Her mom gasses up the car before arriving at the hospital. Then as soon as chemo is over, Helena crawls in the backseat and sleeps while her mom drives the four hours to their home. As long as the car is moving, Helena stays asleep and she doesn't vomit. These four hours of respite get her ready for a long night of nausea and vomiting.

Helping a Parent in Grief

After Barbara's youngest daughter died, Barbara said, "My soul went into hibernation. It was alive but not active. I could have denied the pain, in which case God could never have healed me. I could have rejected my faith, which would have left me nowhere to turn. Or I could go through the pain knowing that I would hold onto my faith and my joy. I've taken this last approach. It may be the most painful of the three initially, but it has given me the foundation I need to survive as a whole and happy person. Walking through my grief was the only way to heal and to care for my other two children."

Barbara's tiny bit of hope during the darkness has sustained her. During her time of retreat she needed steady care, plenty of time to simply be, friends who would listen, and confidence that, though she could not feel it, the joy would return to her life.

Wise Barbara recognized that pain, grief, and suffering are not contrary to Christianity. They're a recognition that people matter. Sadly, rather than friends who understood this, Barbara encountered Christians who tried to explain away her pain with trite phrases like, "God won't put you through more than you can bear," and "At least it's not worse." They misquoted 1 Corinthians 10:13, a verse about temptation, not suffering. Impatient for her to get on with life, they added to Barbara's burden rather than helping her carry it (Galatians 6:2).

One friend understood her need to heal. This friend spent countless hours with Barbara, listening to her, hugging her, getting her out of the house, and helping her with daily chores. She talked with Barbara's children, asking them about school and the other events in their lives. This friend's actions showed confidence that God would heal Barbara.

"We don't have to be super-happy people to express our faith," explained Barbara. "As I healed, I needed to think and feel. At first I couldn't even do that. My friend understood this."

Let people love you well, both during and after your retreat. My favorite source of support is not an organized group or a professional caregiver, but my mother-in-law, with whom I've shared both happy and sad times. She checks with our family, listens, empathizes. She hurts along with us, achieving that delicate balance between becoming overemotional and distancing herself from the pain. She invites us to her home for weekend getaways, caring for the children while my husband and I rest both physically and emotionally. She takes care of us, giving us mother-love in just the way we need it, making us feel safe and at home.

Debbie's friend treated her similarly. As Debbie and her son walked into church for the first time after his cancer diagnosis, a sensitive friend met her at the door and said, "This day will be hard for you, won't it? I just want you to know I'm praying." Her encouraging words brought tears to Debbie's eyes but also empowered her. As hard as it was to go on with life, Debbie knew she had to, for her son's sake and for her own. To do otherwise was to let the cancer and chemotherapy steal the very life Debbie feared losing.

Take your retreat from the pain. Then let those retreats become a part of your life, not a replacement for it. Let your grief and your joy commingle in an unnatural, but effective, mix. Go on with life, confident that God will empower you and your child to face the challenges ahead, and confident that joy does come in the morning (Psalm 30:5).

The Point: As you parent your child through crisis, go through it together. Let nothing, even your own fears, keep you from your child's side during a medical emergency, an illness, or some other physical pain. When the crisis occurs at school or a location where you cannot go, offer your constant support and equip your child with specific skills to manage the crisis.

Application and Reflection:

1. What kind of crisis is happening to your child or perhaps to a friend's child? What are some ways you can help?

2. What fears do you have at this time about this crisis?

3. How will you go through this crisis together? How will you equip your child with skills that will help him (and you) manage this crisis?

4. What lessons have you learned from a previous crisis that could help you deal with future ones? How can you and your child help others who are experiencing similar problems?

5. What Scripture passages have helped you during a crisis? Write these below. Memorize them. Teach them to your child. (Be sure to paraphrase verses for young children so they will understand their meanings.)

About the Writer

Karen Dockrey is the author of more than 28 books. She is the mother of two children who have both faced severe crises. She leads parenting workshops across the U.S. and lives with her family near Nashville, Tennessee. This chapter is from her book, *When a Hug Won't Fix the Hurt: Walking with Your Child Through Crisis* (New Hope Publishers, 2002). Used by permission.